ADAPTIVE WEB DESIGN

Crafting Rich Experiences with
Progressive Enhancement

by Aaron Gustafson

 **easy** readers

Chattanooga, Tennessee

ADAPTIVE WEB DESIGN

Crafting Rich Experiences with Progressive Enhancement

by Aaron Gustafson

Easy Readers, LLC
PO Box 4370
Chattanooga, Tennessee
37405 USA
http://easy-readers.net
Please send errors to errata@easy-readers.net

Editor: Krista Stevens
Project Manager: Kelly McCarthy
Interior Layout: Jessi Taylor
Cover Design: Veerle Pieters
Technical Editors: Craig Cook and Derek Featherstone
Indexer: Jessica Martin

First Edition

Printed and bound in the United States of America

For Kelly

ACKNOWLEDGEMENTS

Without the mentorship and assistance of so many of my friends and colleagues in this industry, not only would this book have never been written, but I would not have been in a position to write it. I'd like to take a moment to extend them my sincerest gratitude:

To Molly Holzschlag and Jeffrey Zeldman for taking me under their wings and helping hone my skills as both a speaker and writer. And to the numerous conference organizers and publications who've given me the opportunity to apply those skills.

To Carolyn Wood for helping shape some of my early drafts and to Krista Stevens for finding the crux of my arguments, streamlining my prose, and taming my inner wiseass.

To Craig Cook and Derek Featherstone for keeping my code on the straight and narrow and to the handful of early reviewers for giving me thoughtful advice (and corrections): Dan Cederholm, Simon Collison, Kristina Halvorson, Christian Heilmann, Whitney Hess, Jeremy Keith, Dan Rubin, and Jonathan Snook.

To the Easy Designs team for their attention to detail and invaluable assistance crafting this book: Jessica Martin, Daniel Ryan, Jessi Taylor, Matthew Turnure, and Laura Helen Winn.

To Veerle Pieters for making time in her busy schedule to design me an absolutely beautiful cover.

And, of course, to Kelly, for finding me the time to write this book, helping me organize my thoughts, and then pushing me to get it done.

TABLE OF CONTENTS

FOREWORD

One glorious afternoon in March, 2006, as a friend and
I hurried past Austin's Downtown Hilton Hotel to catch
the next session of the SXSW Interactive Festival, a young
stranger arrested our progress. With no introduction or
preliminaries, he announced that he was available to speak
at An Event Apart, a conference for web designers that Eric
Meyer and I had launched three months previously. Turning
to my companion with my best impression (which is none too
good) of Mr Burns of "The Simpsons," I asked, "Who is this
brash young upstart, Smithers?"

The brash young upstart quickly became an essential
colleague. In the months and years that followed, Aaron
Gustafson created dazzling front- and back-end code for
some of my agency's most demanding clients. Just as
importantly, he brilliantly tech-edited the third edition of
Designing With Web Standards. The job largely consisted
of alerting Ethan Marcotte and me to the stuff we don't
know about web standards. I'll let you think about that
one. For five years now, Aaron has also been a tough but
fair technical editor for A List Apart magazine, where he
helps authors succeed while ensuring that they are truly
innovative, that their methods are accessible and semantic,
and (thanks to his near-encyclopedic knowledge) that
they give all prior art its due. Moreover, Aaron has written
seminal pieces for the magazine, and, yes, he has lectured at
An Event Apart.

Given my experiences with the man and my admiration for
his knowledge and abilities, I was thrilled when Aaron told
me the premise of this book and began letting me look at
chapters. This isn't just another web design book. It's an
essential and missing piece of the canon. Our industry has
long needed a compendium of best practices in adaptive,
standards-based design. And with the rise of mobile, the

recent significant improvements in desktop and phone browsers, and the new capabilities that come with HTML5, CSS3, and gestural interfaces, it is even more vital that we who make websites have a reliable resource that tells us how to take advantage of these new capabilities while creating content that works in browsers and devices of all sizes and widely differing capabilities. This book is that resource.

The convergence of these new elements and opportunities is encouraging web professionals to finally design for the web as it always should have been done. Adaptive design is the way, and nobody has a wider command than Aaron of the thinking and techniques required to do it well. In these pages you will find all that thinking and those methods. Never again will you lose a day debating how to do great web design (and create great code) that works for everyone. I plan to give this book to all my students, and to everyone I work with. I encourage you to do likewise. And now, enough preliminaries. Dive in, and enjoy!

Jeffrey Zeldman
Author, *Designing With Web Standards 3rd Edition*

CHAPTER 1:
THINK OF THE USER, NOT THE BROWSER

If you've been working on the web for any amount of time, you've likely heard (or even used) the term "progressive enhancement" before. As you probably know, it is the gold standard of how to approach web design. But what is progressive enhancement really? What does it mean? How does it work? And how does it fit into our workflow in a time of rapidly evolving languages and browsers?

These are all good questions and are the very ones I answer throughout this book. As you'll soon see, progressive enhancement isn't about browsers and it's not about which version of HTML or CSS you can use. Progressive enhancement is a philosophy aimed at crafting experiences that serve your users by giving them access to content without technological restrictions.

Cue the kumbayahs, right? It sounds pretty amazing, but it also sounds like a lot of work. Actually, it's not. Once you understand how progressive enhancement works, or more importantly why it works, you'll see it's quite simple.

As we progress through this book you'll see numerous practical ways we can use progressive enhancement in conjunction with HTML, CSS, and JavaScript to create adaptive websites that will not only serve your users well, but provide them with a fantastic experience, no matter what browser or device they are using to access it.

But before we get down to the brass tacks of application, we need to discuss the hows and whys of progressive enhancement, the underpinnings of the philosophy.

ADAPT OR DIE

And when it comes right down to it, progressive enhancement relies on one principle: fault tolerance.

Fault tolerance is a system's ability to continue to operate when it encounters an unexpected error. This property makes it possible for a lizard to regrow its tail and for a brain to reroute neural connections after a trauma. Nature has proven herself quite adept at fault tolerance and, following her example, we've incorporated that concept into our own creations. For example, the oft-lauded "smart grid" can automatically avoid or mitigate power outages by sensing (and in some cases anticipating) system problems.

If you use the web, whether as your professional canvas or simply as a casual consumer, you benefit from fault tolerance all the time. Not only is it baked into the protocols that route a request from your web browser to the server you're trying to reach, it is sewn into the very fabric of the languages that have made the web what it is today: HTML and CSS. As prescribed by the specifications for these two languages, browsers must ignore anything they don't understand. That simple requirement makes progressive enhancement possible. But more on that in a minute.

Another interesting aspect of fault tolerance is how it allows for evolution. Again, looking to nature, you can see this in areas where climate or other environmental factors have caused enough of a change that organisms are forced to adapt, move, or die.

In 1977, the Galapagos Islands experienced a drought that drastically reduced the availability of the small seeds that supported the islands' finch population.[1] Eighty-five percent of the islands' finches were wiped out due to starvation. Oddly enough, it was the larger birds that survived. Why? Because they possessed large beaks capable of cracking the larger, harder seeds that were available. In the absence of a drought, the larger finches possessed no distinct advantage over their smaller relatives, but when the environment changed, they were perfectly positioned to take advantage of the situation and not only survived the drought, but passed their genes along to the next generation of finches which, as you'd expect, tended to be larger.

Public Domain

Figure 1.1: *The varied beaks of Galapagos finches (a.k.a. Darwin's Finches, Geospiza fortis) as seen in The Zoology of the Voyage of H.M.S. Beagle, by John Gould.*

HTML and CSS have a lot in common with the Galapagos finches. Both were designed to be "forward compatible," meaning everything we write today will work tomorrow and next year and in ten years. They are, in a sense, the perfect finch: designed to thrive no matter how the browsing environment itself changes.

These languages were designed to evolve over time, so web browsers were instructed to play by the rules of fault tolerance and ignore anything they didn't understand. This gives these languages room to grow and adapt without ever reaching a point where the content they ensconce and style would no longer be readable or run the risk of causing a browser to crash. Fault tolerance makes it possible to browse an HTML5-driven website in Lynx and allows us to experiment with CSS3 features without worrying about breaking Internet Explorer 6.

Understanding fault tolerance is the key to understanding progressive enhancement. Fault tolerance is the reason progressive enhancement works and makes it possible to ensure all content delivered on the web is accessible and available to everyone.

As fault tolerance has been a component of HTML and CSS since the beginning, you'd think we (as web professionals) would have recognized their importance and value when building our websites. Unfortunately, that wasn't always the case.

"GRACEFUL" MISSTEPS

For nearly a decade after the creation of the web, the medium evolved rapidly. First, the National Center for Supercomputing Applications at the University of Illinois—NCSA for short— gave us Mosaic, the first graphical browser, and HTML got the `img` element. Then came audio. Then video. Then interaction. It was a challenge just to keep up with the rapidly-evolving technology and in our rush to keep up, we lost sight of fault tolerance and began building according to the latest fashion. Some of our sites consisted entirely of full-page image maps layered atop elegantly designed JPEGs. Others became shrines to Macromedia's Flash and Director. Few were usable and even fewer were accessible.

This era gave rise to the development philosophy known as "graceful degradation."

Graceful degradation was the philosophical equivalent of fault tolerance's superficial, image-obsessed sister who is fixated on the latest fashions and only hangs out with the cool kids. As applied to the web, graceful degradation amounted to giving the latest and greatest browsers the experience of a full-course meal, while tossing a few scraps to the sad folk unfortunate enough to be using an older or less-capable browser.

During the heyday of graceful degradation, we focused on making sure our site worked in modern browsers with the greatest market share. Testing for support in older browsers, if we did it at all, was relegated to the end of the list of priorities.

Our reasoning was simple: HTML and CSS are fault tolerant, so at least the user will get something, which (of course) ignored the fact that JavaScript, like other programming languages, is not fault tolerant (i.e., if you try to use a method that doesn't exist, it throws an error); instead, the scripts and applications using JavaScript must be written such that they can either recover from an error (perhaps by trying an alternate method of execution) or predict the potential for an error and exit before it's experienced.

But hardly anyone was doing that because our focus was ever forward as we looked for the next shiny toy we could play with. We assumed that older browsers would have an inferior experience, so we made the justification that it wasn't worth spending the time to ensure it was at least a decent, error-free one. Sure, we'd address the most egregious errors, but beyond that, users were left to fend for themselves. (Sadly, some of us even went so far as to actively block browsers we didn't want to bother supporting.)

THE RISE OF TOLERANCE

Over time, smart folks working on the web began to realize that graceful degradation's emphasis on image over substance was all wrong. They saw that graceful degradation was directly undermining both content availability and accessibility. These designers and developers understood that the web was intended for the distribution and consumption of content— words, images, video, etc.,—and began basing all of their markup, style, and interaction decisions on how each choice would affect the availability of that content.

By refocusing their efforts, developers began to embrace the fault tolerant nature of HTML and CSS as well as JavaScript-based feature detection to enrich a user's experience. They began to realize that a great experience needn't be an all-or-almost-nothing proposition (as was the case under graceful degradation), but instead web technologies could be applied as layers that would build upon one another to create richer experiences and interactions; Steve Champeon of the Web Standards Project perfectly captured the essence of this philosophy when he christened it "progressive enhancement."[1]

Tasty at any level

One analogy I like to use for progressive enhancement is the peanut M&M. At the center of a peanut M&M is, well, the peanut. The peanut itself is a rich source of protein and fat; a

---

1. http://www.hesketh.com/publications/inclusive_web_
    design_for_the_future/

Figure 1.2: *A confectionary continuum.*

great food that everyone can enjoy (except those with an allergy, of course). In a similar sense, the content of our website should be able to be enjoyed without embellishment.

Slather that peanut with some chocolate and you create a mouthwatering treat that, like the peanut, also tastes great. So too, content beautifully organized and arranged using CSS is often easier to understand and certainly more fun to consume.

By coating our nutty confection with a sugary candy shell, the experience of this treat is improved yet again. In a similar sense, we can cap off our beautiful designs with engaging JavaScript-driven interactions that ease our movement through the content or bring it to life in unique and entertaining ways.

This is, of course, an oversimplification of progressive enhancement, but it gives you a general sense of how it works. Technologies applied as layers—HTML, then HTML & CSS, then HTML, CSS & JavaScript—can create different experiences, each one equally valid (and tasty). And at the core of it all is the nut: great content.

The content-out approach

The web is all about information. Every day, on every site, information is disseminated, requested, and collected. Information exchange has been crucial to the growth of the web and will no doubt continue to drive its continued expansion into just about every facet of our daily lives.

As such an important aspect of the web, fostering the exchange of information, should be our primary focus when constructing any web interface. Progressive enhancement ensures that all content (that is to say the information contained in a website) is both available to and usable by anyone, regardless of her location, the device she is using to access that information, or the capabilities of the program she is using to access that content. Similarly, content collection mechanisms—web forms, surveys, and the like— also benefit greatly from progressive enhancement because it ensures they are universally usable and, hence, better at doing their job.

Fundamentally, progressive enhancement is about accessibility, but not in the limited sense the term is most often used. The term "accessibility" is traditionally used to denote making content available to individuals with "special needs" (people with limited motility, cognitive disabilities, or visual impairments); progressive enhancement takes this one step further by recognizing that we all have special needs. Our special needs may also change over time and within different contexts. When I load up a website on my phone, for example, I am visually limited by my screen resolution (especially if I am using a browser that encourages zooming) and I am limited in my ability to interact with buttons and links because I am browsing with my fingertips, which are far larger and less precise than a mouse cursor.

As we've covered, sites built with graceful degradation as their guiding principle may work great in modern browsers, but come up short when viewed in anything less than the latest and greatest browsers for which they were built. In a non-web sense, it puts the user in a position where, like a young child at an amusement park, she may miss out on a great experience because she isn't tall enough to ride the Tilt-a-Whirl. Similarly, users without the "right" browser will likely experience issues (and errors) accessing the site's content, if they can access it at all.

By contrast, a website built following the philosophy of progressive enhancement will be usable by anyone on any device, using any browser. A user on a text-based browser like Lynx won't necessarily have the same experience as a user surfing with the latest version of Safari, but the key is that she will have a positive experience rather than no experience at all. The content of the website will be available to her, albeit with fewer bells and whistles, something that isn't guaranteed with graceful degradation.

While philosophically different, from a practical standpoint progressive enhancement and graceful degradation can look quite similar, which can be confusing. To bring the differences into focus, I like to boil the relationship between the two philosophies down to something akin to standardized testing logic: all experiences that are created using progressive enhancement will degrade gracefully in older browsers, but not all experiences built following graceful degradation are progressively enhanced.

Limits? There are no limits.

During the heyday of graceful degradation, websites became very much like the amusement park I mentioned earlier: "you must be this high to ride." The web was (and, sadly, still is) littered with sites "best viewed in Netscape Navigator 4" and the like. With the rise of progressive enhancement and web standards in general, we moved away from that practice, but as more sites began to embrace the JavaScript technique known as Ajax, the phenomenon resurfaced and many sites began requiring JavaScript or even specific browsers (and browser versions) to view their sites. It was the web's own

B-movie sequel: The Return of the Browser-Breaking, User-Unfriendly Methods We Thought We'd Left Behind.

Over time, the fervor over Ajax died down and we began building (and in some cases rebuilding) Ajax-based sites following the philosophy of progressive enhancement. Then along came Apple's HTML5 Showcase with its pimped out CSS transitions and animations.[2] When we finished wiping the drool off our desks, many of us began incorporating these shiny new toys into our work, either because of our eagerness to play with these features or at our clients' behest. Consequently, sites began cropping up that restricted users by requiring a modern Webkit variant[3] in order to run. (Damn the nearly 80% of browsers that didn't include.)

When self-realization hit that requiring technologies that are not universally available ran counter to progressive enhancement, some web designers and developers declared the philosophy "limiting" and began drifting back toward graceful degradation. Progressive enhancement, they felt, forced them to focus on serving older browsers which, frankly, weren't nearly as fun to work with. What they failed to realize, however, was that progressive enhancement wasn't limiting them; their own understanding of the philosophy was.

---

2. http://www.apple.com/html5/

3. Webkit is the engine that powers a number of browsers and applications. It has excellent CSS support and boasts support for quite a few snazzy CSS capabilities (such as CSS-based animations) yet to be matched by other browsers. Webkit can be found in Apple's Safari, Google's Chrome and Android browsers, the Symbian S60 browser, Shiira, iCab, OmniWeb, Epiphany, and many other browsers. It forms the basis for Palm's WebOS operating system and has been integrated into numerous Adobe products including their Adobe Integrated Runtime (AIR) and the CS5 application suite.

Progressive enhancement isn't about browsers. It's about crafting experiences that serve your users by giving them access to content without technological restrictions. Progressive enhancement doesn't require that you provide the same experience in different browsers, nor does it preclude you from using the latest and greatest technologies; it simply asks that you honor your content (and your users) by applying technologies in an intelligent way, layer-upon-layer, to craft an amazing experience. Browsers and technologies will come and go. Marrying progressive enhancement with your desire to be innovative and do incredible things in the browser is entirely possible, as long as you're smart about your choices and don't lose sight of your users.

Progressive enhancement = excellent customer service

Imagine, for a moment, that you are a waiter in a nice restaurant. Your job (and your tip) depends upon your attention to detail and how well you serve your customers. One measure of your attentiveness is how empty you let a customer's water glass become before refilling it. An inattentive waiter might let the glass sit empty for several minutes before refilling it. Someone slightly more on the ball might only let it hit the halfway mark before topping it up. A waiter who excels at meeting his customer's beverage needs would not only make sure the water level never fell even that far, but he would even manage to refill the glass without the customer even realizing it. Whose customers do you think walk away the most satisfied? And, if we're judging solely based on satisfactory hydration, who do you think is likely to get the best tip?

As web designers and developers, we should strive to be as good at our job as that attentive, unobtrusive waiter, but it isn't a simple task. Just as a waiter has no idea if a customer coming through the door will require frequent refills or few, we have no way of knowing a particular user's needs when they arrive on our site. Instead, we must rise to meet those needs. If we're really good, we can do so without our customers even realizing we're making special considerations for them. Thankfully, with progressive enhancement's user and content-focused approach (as opposed to graceful degradation's newest-browser approach), this is easily achievable.

RISING TO THE OCCASION

When approaching a project from a progressive enhancement perspective, your core focus is the content and everything builds upon that. It's a layered approach that rises to meet a user's "needs" by paying attention to the context within which a page is accessed (a combination of the browser's capabilities and, to a lesser extent, the medium in which it is operating) and adapting the user experience accordingly.

The baseline experience is always in the form of text. No specific technology shapes this layer, instead its success or failure relies entirely on the skills of the copywriter. Clear, well-written copy has universal device support and does wonders to improve the accessibility of the content to users. Furthermore, no matter how the HTML language evolves over time, the imperative that browsers be fault tolerant in their treatment of HTML syntax ensures that, no matter what, the content it describes will always be available in its most basic form: as text.

The second level of experience comes from the semantics of the HTML language itself. The various elements and attributes used on a page provide additional meaning and context to the written words. They indicate important notions such as emphasis and provide supplementary information, such as the source of a quote or the meaning of an unfamiliar phrase.

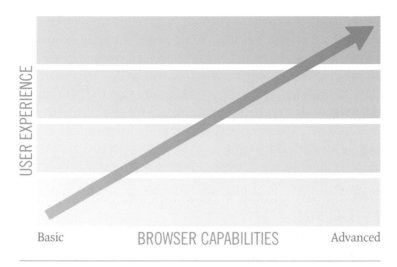

Figure 1.3: *Graph of progressive enhancement*

The third level of experience is the audio-visual one, expressed through the use of CSS and the use of inline images, audio, and video. As with HTML, implementations of CSS within a browser are necessarily fault tolerant, so browsers ignore that which they don't understand; a fact that makes progressive enhancement in CSS a possibility.

The fourth level of experience is the interactive one. In the standards world, this level relies almost entirely on JavaScript, though interaction on the web has been realized through other technologies such as Flash or even Java applets.

The final level is realized through the application of enhanced semantics and best practices contained within and used in conjunction with the Web Accessibility Initiative's Accessible Rich Internet Applications (WAI-ARIA) spec. These enhancements to the page pick up where the HTML spec has traditionally left off (though HTML5 does include some of the enhanced ARIA semantics in its lexicon).

These levels of experience (which can also be thought of as levels of support), when stacked upon one another, create an experience that grows richer with each step, but they are by no means the only experiences that will be had by a user. In fact, they are simply identifiable milestones on the path from the most basic experience to the most exceptional one. A user's actual experience may vary at one or more points along the path and that's alright; as long as we keep progressive enhancement in mind, our customers will be well served.

LET'S DIG IN

The remainder of this book will take you on a tour of the various mile markers on the progressive enhancement highway, starting with markup and continuing through CSS, JavaScript and, finally, ARIA. Along the way, we'll examine the application of progressive enhancement techniques on an event page found on Retreats4Geeks.com. By design, this book is not intended to be an exhaustive compendium of progressive enhancement techniques, so the examples will be brief and focused, exposing you to current best practices and jump-starting your use of progressive enhancement in your own work.

Figure 1.4: *The event page from Retreats4Geeks.com that we will be dissecting throughout this book.*

"The meaning is in the content of the text and not in the typeface."

— WIM CROUWEL

CHAPTER 2:
PROGRESSIVE ENHANCEMENT WITH MARKUP

When it comes to the web, markup calls the shots. It is the foundation upon which every beautiful design and each amazing experience is built. Whether your preferred flavor is HTML or its more rigorous sibling, XHTML, each element has a purpose and can profoundly affect the user experience for better or worse, depending on how you use (or abuse) it.

FROM A ROUGH START TO THE RIGHT WAY™

When we first began building web pages, many of us misunderstood the importance of good markup. Those of us coming to the web from a programming background often considered learning HTML beneath us, so we never put in the time to come to grips with the semantics it provided. Those of us who came to the web from a design background didn't understand the importance of semantics either. We thought only of the presentational aspect of a web page and latched on to the `table` as a means of laying out pages on a grid, then we went hog-wild and found hundreds of other uses for the `table` element, many of which supplanted existing (and well-supported) semantic elements (like lists).

In many offices across the globe, advocacy for semantic application of HTML fell on deaf ears; the argument was seen as a largely idealistic one because: 1) the fact remained that old-school websites looked okay in modern browsers and 2) the case for greater web accessibility was lost on many people who had no first-hand experience of using the web with a disability. Then Google came along and changed everything. Suddenly, semantic markup was important.

Google was the first search engine to take semantics into account when indexing web pages. Starting with the humble anchor (`a`) element, the cornerstone of their original PageRank algorithm, Google pioneered the use of semantic markup to infer meaning and relevancy. The other search engines soon followed and, as search engine spiders began hunting for other meaningful HTML elements on web pages (e.g., `h1` which indicates the most important content on a page), semantic markup became more important to the business world because proper use of it meant a better ranking in search engines and, thereby, a greater opportunity to attract new customers.

THE SEMANTIC FOUNDATION

If content were soil, semantic markup would be the compost you'd add to ensure a productive garden. It enriches the content, providing your users with clues about intent and context, as well as supplementary information about the content itself.

Take, for example, the abbreviation element (`abbr`). It is used to denote abbreviations (and acronyms, now that it has officially replaced the `acronym` element):

```
Gatlinburg, <abbr title="Tennessee">TN</abbr>
```

In this simple HTML snippet, you can see how the abbreviation enhances the letters "TN" by informing the user that they stand for "Tennessee."

As HTML has evolved, its vocabulary has steadily expanded to offer more options for describing the content it encapsulates. The advent of HTML5 ushered in a slew of new semantic options (such as `header`) and even augmented a few existing ones (such as the aforementioned `abbr` that took over for the ousted `acronym`). As we proceed through this chapter, we'll employ several of these new/revised elements and I will provide a little background about why they are an appropriate choice for marking up content.

Let's get started.

SAYING WHAT WE MEAN

Looking at the Retreats 4 Geeks web page[1], it may be hard to figure out where to start, but we'll begin with the most important content: the name of the site and the links to the various sections of the page (since this is, for our purposes, a single-page website).

Figure 2.1: *A screen shot of the site highlighting the site name and navigation elements*

---

1. If you haven't already downloaded the sample files, you can do so by visiting adaptivewebdesign.info

Let's consider this component from a semantician's point of view, starting with the logo. The Retreats 4 Geeks logo is an image, so we should use an `img` element to mark it up.[2] It's also pretty important because it provides a context for the entire page, so it should be wrapped in an `h1`, an element reserved for the most important content on a page:

```
<h1><img src="i/logo.png"/></h1>
```

Though the example page is written using HTML5, I've always been more comfortable with the XML serialization of the language, so I've chosen to stick with that syntax (as evidenced by the trailing slash on the `img` element). It is more a matter of preference than requirement.

Moving on to the navigation, we're presenting a list of links, so it should be marked up as such. As the order of the links corresponds to the order of the sections on the page, the list should probably be of the ordered variety (`ol`). Each link gets placed in a list item (`li`) and wrapped in an anchor element (`a`):

```
<ol>
  <li><a href="#details">Details</a></li>
  <li><a href="#schedule">Schedule</a></li>
  <li><a href="#instructors">Instructors</a></li>
  <li><a href="#lodging">Lodging</a></li>
  <li><a href="#location">Location</a></li>
</ol>
```

Up until this point, we've made the obvious choices with regard to markup, employing semantics we've had in HTML since the beginning. Just over a year ago, we would have likely stopped here and considered the header complete, but HTML5 gives us the opportunity to improve both the semantic value and the accessibility of this content.

---

2.   Yeah, I know, you could also use the `object` element or make it text and use CSS to replace it with an image, but we're going for simplicity here.

Traditionally, we might have employed a page division (div) with a semantic identifier (id) of "header" to contain these two elements. Divisions, as you'll recall, are used to group content, but they provide no context as to the purpose or function of that group (which is why we would identify it as the "header"). HTML5, however, introduces an element that provides the explicit semantic meaning for that division: header.

Semantically, a header is used to demarcate any content that is summarily important to a page or section of a page. It can be used to encapsulate headings or heading groups (contained in the new hgroup element), relevant navigational aids, and introductory content. As such, it makes a perfect container for the title of our page and the list of anchors to each article within the page.

HTML5 also grants us another more appropriate option when it comes to the navigation. Whereas we would have traditionally identified the ordered list as "nav" or "main-nav," HTML5's nav element more directly expresses the semantics we're trying to imbue the ol with by providing that semantic id. The nav element can be used to wrap any group of navigational links and functions as the semantic equivalent of the ARIA landmark role of "navigation" (which we'll discuss more in Chapter 5).

With these additions, the markup for this section is now:

```
<header>
  <h1><img src="i/logo.png"/></h1>
  <nav>
   <ol>
     <li><a href="#details">Details</a></li>
     <li><a href="#schedule">Schedule</a></li>
     <li><a href="#instructors">Instructors</a></li>
```

```
    <li><a href="#lodging">Lodging</a></li>
    <li><a href="#location">Location</a></li>
  </ol>
  </nav>

</header>
```

And, thanks to the fact that they ignore anything they don't understand, the markup we've used will work in every browser, regardless of age. Sure, modern browsers may treat the newer elements differently, but even text-based browsers (such as Lynx) will be able to access the content. Devoid of style and stripped of JavaScript-based interactivity, the markup just works, providing us with the second level of support in the progressive enhancement continuum. (Remember: the content itself forms the crucial first level).

INVISIBLE AND ADVISORY

As good as this markup is, we've neglected a major accessibility requirement by not providing any alternate text for our logo image (expressed using the alt attribute). "Alt text," as it's most often known,[3] provides a text-based back-up for users who have images turned off; it is also the content that is read to users of screen reading software (such as the blind), which is why its inclusion is critical.

Returning to the example, I've added a simple alt attribute:

```
<h1><img src="i/logo.png" alt="Retreats 4
  Geeks"/></h1>
```

---

3. Some people get very grumpy when they hear the term "alt tag" because tags and attributes are very different things (attributes are applied to the opening tag of an element). If you ever find yourself starting to pronounce a "t" after saying "alt," catch yourself and roll right into "text." "Alt attribute" is a bit of a mouthful anyway.

When the image in question is a logo or conveys information needed to understand the page or accomplish key tasks, `alt` text should always be supplied. For all other images, it's perfectly legitimate to leave the `alt` text blank (`alt=""`). I would even go so far as to say it's *advisable* to use an empty `alt` attribute in any instance where the image doesn't supply necessary information. I say this for two reasons: 1) no one really wants to read vacuous copy like "Smiling man throws a Frisbee to a leaping Golden Retriever" any more than someone else wants to write it; and 2) screen readers will speak the contents of the `alt` attribute aloud, but will skip any images with empty `alt` attributes.[4]

Whereas the `alt` attribute is used to provide alternative content, the `title` attribute is used to provide advisory information about an element. In the case of the navigation links in the above example, we can use `title` to provide the user with information about where each link will take her:

```
<li><a href="#location" title="Get the 411 on
   Gatlinburg, Tennessee">Location</a></li>
```

Similarly, further down the page in the "location" section, `title` provides context to the link that wraps the map:

```
<a href="http://maps.google.com/..." title="View
   Gatlinburg, Tennessee on Google Maps">
   <img src="http://maps.google.com/..." alt="A map
      showing the location of Gatlinburg, Tennessee"/>
</a>
```

---

4. A screen reader will actually say "image" each time it encounters an `img` lacking an `alt` attribute, so be kind to screen reader users and don't forget to include them.

35°43'19"N 83°29'58"W

Figure 2.2: *A screen shot of the location portion of the page with a cursor over the map.*

AD-HOC SEMANTICS

HTML is filled with attributes that help enrich the elements they adorn. It prescribes a number of "fixed use" ones, like `alt` and `title`, but it also offers a handful of attributes that can be used to build upon the language's native semantics in a less formal way. I'm talking, of course, about `id` and `class`.

When Dave Raggett drafted a specification for HTML 3.0,[5] it contained two new concepts: classification and identification, expressed via the `class` and `id` attributes respectively.[6] These

5. HTML 3.0 was an ambitious spec, introducing numerous tags and attributes. Many of those new constructs were dropped by the time it reached recommendation status as HTML 3.2, but the `class` and `id` attributes survived. Funny enough, some of the very same constructs proposed in HTML 3.0 have found their way back into the HTML lexicon, either formally as part of HTML5 or quasi-formally as microformats.

6. It's worth noting that `class` and `id` each make a (very) brief appearance in the HTML 2 spec (`http://www.ietf.org/rfc/rfc1866.txt`), but were not formally-defined attributes. They were simply used to demonstrate the fault tolerant way in which browsers should treat unknown attributes.

two attributes were not formally introduced into the HTML lexicon until HTML 4.0, but were implemented in browsers around the same time as Cascading Style Sheet (CSS) support was added. And CSS, of course, brought us two simple selectors that targeted these attributes explicitly, causing some unfortunate confusion over the intended use of class and id from the get-go.

For years, nearly every web developer working with CSS thought the correlation between the attributes and the selectors was intentional, believing that id and class were intended purely for use with style sheets. You can hardly blame us though, CSS Level 1 did not provide many mechanisms for selecting elements, so it made sense that the class selector (e.g., ul.menu) and the id selector (e.g., div#content) would have been introduced (along with their corresponding attributes) for the purposes of both the general and specific application of style, respectively.[7]

Thankfully, we now understand how the class and id attributes were meant to operate. The class attribute was introduced specifically to address the limited set of elements within the HTML lexicon:

> As time goes by, people's expectations change, and more will be demanded of HTML. One manifestation of this is the pressure to add yet more tags. HTML 3.0 introduces a means for subclassing elements in an open-ended way. This can be used to distinguish the role of a paragraph element as being a couplet in a stansa [sic], or a mathematical term as being a tensor. This ability to make fresh distinctions can be exploited to impart distinct rendering styles or to support richer search mechanisms, without further complicating the HTML document format itself.[8]

---

7. And the HTML 3 draft did allow for this use, among others. The draft is available at http://www.w3.org/MarkUp/html3/html3.txt.

8. From the "Scalability" section of the HTML 3 draft (see footnote 7).

The intent was that this attribute would contain a list of subclasses for the particular element they were applied to, with the classes listed from most general to most specific:[9]

```
<a href="…" title="…">
  <img class="illustration map" src="…" alt="…"/>
</a>
```

The spec introduced the id attribute for the purposes of identifying a specific element on the page (this is why each id on a page needs to be unique). In practice, this identifier would be used as a reference point for style rules (#details { … }), scripts (document.getElementById('details')), and anchors (<a href="#details">). You may recall that we actually used that last mechanism in the navigation introduced earlier in the chapter.

As all of the information for the Retreats 4 Geeks event is included on a single page, I've grouped each chunk of content into separate article elements[10], each with a unique id. The article element was introduced as part of HTML5 and demarcates content that forms an independent part of the document, such as a newspaper article, blog post, or, in our case, a distinct topic. Each of the articles on the page is then targeted, using its id as an anchor reference, by the navigation links. Clicking one of these links will jump a user directly to the appropriate content:

---

9. You'll see this throughout the HTML 3 draft, whenever class is defined for an element.

10. Not to be confusing, but HTML5 also introduces the section element (also seen in the above code example). In HTML5 parlance, the section element denotes a *section* of content (go figure, right?). In terms of overall organization, I could have declared the whole page an article, making each distinct chunk a section of that article, but I decided that individual article elements made more sense because each chunk of content is independent enough that it could easily exist on its own page. The semantic difference between the two is modest at best and the choice of one over the other is really at the discretion of the author.

```
<body>
  <header>

    <h1><img src="/2010/retreat-js/i/logo.png"
    alt="Retreats 4 Geeks"/></h1>

    <nav>
     <ol>
       <li><a href="#details" title="Find out what
         this retreat is all about">Details</a></li>
       <li><a href="#schedule" title="Get familiar
         with what this retreat will cover">Schedule
         </a></li>
       ...
     </ol>
    </nav>

  </header>
  <div id="content">

    <article id="details">...</article>
    <article id="schedule">...</article>
    ...

  </div>
</body>
```

The class and id attributes allow page authors to create
their own semantics on top of those that are part of the
spec. Together, these ad-hoc semantics imbue the markup
with greater meaning and, over time, have gravitated toward
a common set of classifications and identifiers in use across
the globe (e.g., div#header and ul#nav). This common
set of classifications and identifiers has, in turn, provided
valuable feedback in the development of the HTML language
itself (resulting in additions like HTML5's header and
nav elements, which we reviewed earlier) and fostered the
development of a community-driven set of extensions to
HTML known as "microformats."

CODIFIED CONVENTIONS

Microformats are a set of community-driven specifications for how to mark up content to expose semantics (and meta data) that are not available in HTML (or XHTML). At their essence, microformats formalize organically-developed coding conventions into a specification that addresses an oversight or limitation in HTML. For example, HTML provides no robust way to mark up contact information or events, so the community created microformats to fill those needs.

The first microformat arose from a desire to express associations between individuals on the web and was called the XHTML Friends Network ("XFN" for short). Though not developed as a "microformat" (that term came later), XFN was a perfect example of extending the semantics of HTML with a specific goal in mind.

Developed by Tantek Çelik, Matthew Mullenweg, and Eric Meyer, XFN makes use of the oft-neglected rel attribute. The purpose of rel—which you are probably familiar with in the context of the link element for inclusion of an external stylesheet (rel="stylesheet")—is to indicate the relationship of the target of an anchor to the current page. The idea was simple: if I wanted to point from my blog to the blog of a colleague, I could employ XFN and add rel="colleague" to the link. Similarly, if I was linking to my wife's blog, I would use rel="friend co-resident spouse muse sweetheart co-worker" because she is all of those things.[11]

On its own, this additional markup does little more than provide a bit more information about our relationship and why I might be linking to another website, but if I use it for every link in my blog roll and those people, in turn, use it in theirs, all of a sudden we've created a network that is

11. Awwww.

navigable programmatically, creating myriad opportunities for data mining and repurposing. And that's exactly what happened: XFN spread like wildfire. Software developers integrated it into popular blogging tools (e.g., WordPress, Movable Type) and developers at nearly every site on the "social web" (e.g., Twitter , Flickr, Last.fm) began adorning user profile pages with the special case of rel="me" (used to link from one web page you control to another), enabling tools like Google's Social Graph to quickly build a full profile of their users starting from a single URL.[12]

An example of XFN in the Retreats 4 Geeks page can be found in the footer[13]:

```
<footer>

  <p id="copyright">&copy;2010 Retreats 4 Geeks. All
  Rights Reserved.</p>

  <p>Retreats 4 Geeks is an <a rel="me"
  href="http://easy-designs.net/">Easy! Designs
  </a> venture.</p>

</footer>
```

From that simple (yet powerful) beginning, microformats have increased in number to address common and diverse needs from marking up a person's profile (hCard), event listings (hCalendar), content for syndication (hAtom), and resumes (hResume), to indicating license information

---

12. More on the Social Graph API can be found at http://code. google.com/apis/socialgraph/. Glenn Jones uses this API in the fantastic JavaScript library Ident Engine (http://identengine. com/), which he introduced in the pages of A List Apart (http:// www.alistapart.com/articles/discovering-magic/).

13. The footer element is another product of the HTML5 spec and is intended to encapsulate "meta" information about an article, section, or page such as the author, copyright information, and so forth.

(rel-license), controlling search engine spidering (rel-nofollow), and facilitating tagging (rel-tag).[14]

Almost in parallel with the development of these microformats, numerous tools sprung up to make use of them. As you can probably guess from my mention of the Google Social Graph, search engines have started to pay attention to microformats and, in some cases, even rank microformatted content higher than non-microformatted content. Browser add-ons-such as Operator[15] and Oomph[16] enable users to extract and repurpose microformatted content. Microformat parsers are also available for nearly every programming language and there are even web-based services, such as Optimus[17] and H2VX[18], that give users more direct access to the microformats in use on their sites.

As you can see, microformats are yet another layer in the progressive enhancement continuum, enabling us to make our sites even more useful to our users. After all, how cool is it that, using a tool like Operator or a service like Optimus, we can enable users to import an event to their calendar or a business card to their address book directly from our web page? I think that's pretty awesome.

Call me, call me anytime

As our demo website is for an event, the hCalendar microformat is an obvious place to start, but let's hold off on that for a moment and look at how we can apply the

---

14. The microformats wiki (http://microformats.org/wiki/) keeps a running list of all microformats and documentation on how to use them.

15. http://kaply.com/weblog/operator/

16. http://visitmix.com/labs/oomph/

17. http://microformatique.com/optimus/

18. http://h2vx.com/

hCard microformat to my bio `section` in the "Instructors" `article`. Before we take a look at the markup though, let's go over the key hCard classifications.

CLASS	PURPOSE
vcard	Signifies that hCard is being used. (This should be the class of the root element containing the hCard information.)
fn	Short for "formatted name," it's used to wrap the name of the person who owns the hCard
url	Indicates that a given link takes the user to a web page about this person
photo	Denotes a photo of this person
org	Identifies the company or organization of which this person is a part
role	Conveys the role this person holds within the organization

Table 2.1: *Key hCard classifications*

The hCard microformat offers many other options for marking up a person's profile, but these are the key ones we're going to concern ourselves within the context of the Retreats 4 Geeks website. And, of these five `classes`, only "vcard" and "fn" are actually required.

Now let's take a look at the content we've got to work with:

```
<section id="aaron-gustafson">

  <figure>
   <img src="i/aaron-gustafson.jpg" alt=""/>
  </figure>

  <h1>Aaron Gustafson</h1>
```

<p>Aaron has been working on the web for nearly 15 years and, in that time, has cultivated a love of web standards and an in-depth knowledge of website strategy and architecture, interface design, and numerous languages (including XHTML, CSS, JavaScript, and PHP). Aaron and his wife, Kelly, own <a rel="external" href="http://easy-designs.net">Easy! Designs</a>, a boutique web consultancy based in Chattanooga, TN. When not neck deep in code, Aaron is usually found evangelizing his findings and sharing his knowledge and passion with others in the field.</p>

<p>Aaron has trained professionals at <cite>The New York Times</cite>, Gartner, and the US Environmental Protection Agency (among others), and has presented at the world's foremost web conferences, such as An Event Apart and Web Directions. He is Group Manager of the <a rel="external" href="http://webstandards.org">Web Standards Project (WaSP)</a> and serves as an Invited Expert to the World Wide Web Consortium's <a rel="external" href="http://www.w3.org/2005/Incubator/owea/">Open Web Education Alliance (OWEA)</a>. He created <a rel="external" href="http://ecsstender.org">eCSStender</a>, serves as Technical Editor for <a rel="external" href="http://alistapart.com"><cite>A List Apart</cite></a>, is a contributing writer for <a rel="external" href="http://netmag.co.uk"><cite>.net Magazine</cite></a>, and has filled a small library with his technical writing and editing credits. His next book, <cite>Adaptive Web Design: Crafting Rich Experiences with Progressive Enhancement</cite>, is due out in early 2011.</p>

</section>

You probably noticed that the section has an h1 as its title. Don't worry: in HTML5, each section creates a new context within which it's okay to restart the headings at h1. It takes a little getting used to at first, I know, but it makes sense and addresses the limited number of heading levels quite well.[19]

If you've got keen eyes, you've likely already identified exactly where each of the hCard classes should be applied, but I'll step through each one, just to be sure, starting with the easiest one: "vcard." This classification needs to be applied to the containing element, in this case, the section:

```
<section id="aaron-gustafson" class="vcard">
```

The next obvious one is "fn," which should wrap my name. As my name is already wrapped in an h1, we can apply a class of "fn" to that element to indicate the text contained within the element is my name.

```
<h1 class="fn">Aaron Gustafson</h1>
```

Next, we can add a class of "url" to the "Easy! Designs" link, denoting that it points to a website I control:

```
... <a class="url" rel="external" href="http://easy-
designs.net">Easy! Designs</a>, ...
```

Continuing down the list, we can apply "photo" to the image of me, which is contained in a figure element. HTML5 introduced the figure element to contain a discrete chunk of content—usually an image or graphic with an optional caption (figcaption)—that can stand on its own or be removed from a document without altering its meaning:

```
<figure>
  <img class="photo" src="i/aaron-gustafson.jpg"
    alt=""/>
</figure>
```

19. http://www.whatwg.org/specs/web-apps/current-work/
    multipage/content-models.html#sectioning-content

We need to add the two final classes, "org" and "role" to this markup in the final paragraph of my bio, but the content presents us with a bit of a conundrum as there are several roles and organizations mentioned. Which one should we use? Is it okay to include multiple organizations and roles?

There is nothing in the hCard spec that restricts an hCard to a singular organization and role, but, in practice, few microformats parsers will expose anything beyond the first one encountered because address book software doesn't typically allow for multiple organizations and roles. For that reason, we'll simply add the classification to my primary function: Group Manager of the Web Standards Project.

The "org" bit is easy because "Web Standards Project" is already contained in an element. My role there, however, is part of a larger text string and is not contained within its own element. To apply the classification to my role only, we have to make use of an element bereft of semantic meaning, such as b:[20]

```
… He is <b class="role">Group Manager</b> of the
<a class="org" href="http://webstandards.org">Web
Standards Project (WaSP)</a> …
```

Viewed all at once, you can see that the adjustments to incorporate the hCard microformat are quite minimal:

```
<section id="aaron-gustafson" class="vcard">

  <figure>
    <img class="photo" src="/events/2011/html5-
    css3/i/aaron-gustafson.jpg" alt=""/>
  </figure>
```

---

20. What? b? Really? Why not span? Well, in HTML5, the b element has been brought back for the explicit purpose of representing "a span of text to be stylistically offset from the normal prose without conveying any extra importance." While you can certainly use the span element, b is a more appropriate (and shorter) alternative.

```
<h1 class="fn">Aaron Gustafson</h1>

<p>… Aaron and his wife, Kelly, own <a class="url"
   rel="external" href="http://easy-designs.
   net">Easy! Designs</a> …</p>

<p>… He is <b class="role">Group Manager</b> of
   the <a class="org" rel="external" href="http://
   webstandards.org">Web Standards Project
   (WaSP)</a> …</p>

</section>
```

But these simple changes allow a microformats parser to put together a profile of me quite easily.

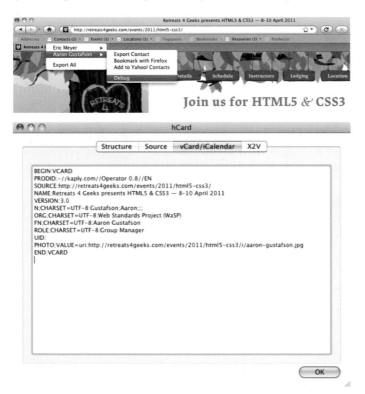

Figure 2.3: *Screen shots of the information exposed from this code via Operator.*

What's really interesting about microformats is that you can use them however you like. The `class` names don't need to appear in any particular order (so long as they appear within an appropriately-classified parent element) and they don't require that the content match the intended export format in any way. And, as this example demonstrates, the hCard does not need to be marked up like a rolodex card entry; instead, you are free to sprinkle its component parts throughout your prose using the appropriate `class` names to indicate each one.

Mark your calendars

With hCard covered, we can take a look at the hCalendar event microformat mentioned earlier. Again, before we look at the markup, let's take a look at some of the more important hCalendar classifications.

CLASS	PURPOSE
vevent	Signifies that an hCalendar event is being used. (This should be the `class` of the root element containing the hCalendar event information.)
dtstart	Indicates the start date of the event
dtend	Denotes the end date of the event
summary	Identifies the name of the event
location	States the location of the event
description	Provides additional details about the event

Table 2.2: *Important hCalender classifications*

As the entire demo page is dedicated to the event, the `class`-application process needs to begin further up the DOM tree. I've decided to start at the content container (`div#content`), to which I've assigned the root "vevent" `class`. While in the following example, the hCalendar content is contained within `article#details`, applying the `class` to an ancestor element in this manner gives us the flexibility to include more hCalendar properties in the other `articles` as well:

```
<div id="content" class="vevent">
```

As I mentioned, the first article (`article#details`) contains the bulk of the information about the event. Let's take a look at that markup before we review the application of the hCalendar classes:

```
<article id="details">

  <header>

    <h1>Join us for HTML5 &amp; CSS3</h1>

    <p>8&#8211;10 April 2011</p>

    <p>Gatlinburg, <abbr title="Tennessee">TN</
      abbr></p>

  </header>

  <figure>
    <img src="i/mountains.jpg" alt=""/>
  </figure>

  <section class="main">
    <!-- event overview -->
  </section>

</article><!-- / #details -->
```

Glancing over the markup, you've probably already figured out where most of the hCalendar classifications should be applied. Right off the bat, you have the name of the event or "summary" in hCalendar parlance:

```
<h1>Join us for <b class="summary">HTML5 &amp;
CSS3</b></h1>
```

In terms of source order, the next piece we encounter is the date range "8–10 April 2011." Traditionally, we would have used abbreviation elements (abbr) to mark up this data, but HTML5 introduces a new element explicitly tasked with indicating temporal information: the time element. One problem: to supply a start and end date for the event, we need to break the content up into two dates before wrapping each in a time element.

Though it may seem odd at first, what makes the most sense is wrapping the "8" in one time element and "10 April 2011" in the other. We do that because the "8" is really implying "8 April 2011," albeit in an abbreviated form (which is why abbr made a lot of sense previously). The time element allows for further clarification of dates using the datetime attribute, which is how I've expressed the full starting date:

```
<p><time datetime="2011-04-08">8</
time>&#8211;<time datetime="2011-04-10">10 April
2011</time></p>
```

hCalendars only require a summary and a starting date, so we only need to apply the "dtstart" classification to the first time element for the microformat to be valid. But since we have an end date, it makes sense to apply that one too:[21]

```
<p><time class="dtstart" datetime="2011-04-08">8</
time>&#8211;<time class="dtend"
datetime="2011-04-10">10 April 2011</time></p>
```

Continuing down the article, "location" is pretty obvious: Gatlinburg, TN:

```
<p class="location">Gatlinburg, <abbr
title="Tennessee">TN</abbr></p>
```

---

21. As of this writing, some microformat parsers have issues with the newer HTML5 elements and attributes. For that reason, it may make sense to duplicate the value of the datetime attribute into a title on the time element or switch to using title on an abbr.

The final piece of our hCalendar puzzle is the "description" and the most obvious choice of content for that property is the "main" section of the article:

```
<section class="main description">
  <!-- event overview -->
</section>
```

And that's it. With the microformatted content in place, it's now quite simple for users to export the event directly to their calendar.

Figure 2.4: *Screen shots of the information exposed from this code via Operator.*

Again, we've seen how microformats can directly enhance the meaning of already meaningful markup in order to improve the user experience. Picture perfect progressive enhancement!

IT'S THE FOUNDATION

While progressive enhancement is often discussed in terms of CSS and JavaScript, it applies equally to the markup. As we've seen in this chapter, every time we choose a meaningful element, we make it easier for the page to do its job by enhancing accessibility and increasing its visibility to potential users through organic search. We've also seen how both classification and identification can feed back into HTML, helping it become an even more expressive language. And, as is the case with microformats, we've even seen how the names we choose have the capacity to enhance both the semantics and usability of the content to which they are applied.

Semantic markup is an invaluable step in the progressive enhancement continuum; in concert with well written content, it forms the foundation upon which the entire user experience is built.

"Design is the fundamental soul of a human-made creation that ends up expressing itself in successive outer layers of the product or service."

— STEVE JOBS

CHAPTER 3:
PROGRESSIVE ENHANCEMENT WITH CSS

With the possible exception of a few straggling websites still limping along with their font elements and spacer GIFs, design on the web is largely accomplished using Cascading Style Sheets (CSS). Sure, there's Flash, SVG, and canvas, but if you are concerned about the availability and accessibility of your content, you're going to be using HTML to mark up your content and CSS to style it.

As with HTML, CSS is designed to be fault tolerant. Browsers ignore any syntax they don't understand[1, 2] and, by paying attention to how the language has evolved over time, we can easily embrace progressive enhancement by taking advantage of this ignorance to craft layers of design based on a given browser's capabilities.

---

1. http://www.w3.org/TR/2009/CR-CSS2-20090908/syndata. html#parsing-errors
2. http://www.w3.org/TR/2009/CR-CSS2-20090908/syndata. html#unsupported-values

SOMETIMES AN ERROR CAN BE A GOOD THING

This isn't a CSS book, so I'm not going to walk you through all of the options available to you in CSS. One thing I do want to do, however, is give you an ever-so-brief recap of how CSS works because I think it will provide you with invaluable insight into how to construct progressive designs.

At its most fundamental, CSS is a series of human-readable rule sets, each composed of a selector and declaration block containing a set of property-value pairs (declarations) to be applied to any element matched by the selector.

```
p {
  color: red;
  font-weight: bold;
}
```

The example above is about as basic as CSS gets. Anyone who's worked with CSS before (and probably even someone who hasn't) can look at it and quickly comprehend that it selects paragraphs and makes their text bold and red. Looking at this example through the lens of fault tolerance, however, you'll see things a little differently.

When parsing a CSS file to determine how to render a page, a browser reads each rule set and examines it. If it encounters something it doesn't understand, it experiences something we call a "parsing error." Parsing errors are often the result of malformed CSS syntax (e.g., the misspelling of a property name or value, a missing colon or semicolon, etc.), but they also result when perfectly valid CSS syntax is beyond the parser's comprehension.

Assuming all of our curly braces, colons, and semicolons are in their proper places, the example we just saw contains five points at which a parsing error could occur:

① p { **②**   **③**
    color: red;
    font-weight: bold;
  }   **④**   **⑤**

1. the selector: p;
2. the first property name: color;
3. the value of the first property: "red";
4. the second property name: font-weight; and
5. the value assigned to the second property: "bold."

According to the specification, if a browser encounters this rule set and doesn't understand a part of it (i.e., it experiences a parsing error), the browser must ignore the larger component of the rule set in which the parsing error occurs.

So, for example, if the browser did not understand the CSS color keyword "red," it would ignore the declaration color: red, but would still apply the remaining declarations. The same goes for the font-weight keyword "bold." If, however, the browser was unable to understand the selector (p), it would ignore the entire rule set, regardless of the browser's ability to comprehend the individual declarations it contained.

The reasoning behind this is simple: We don't know what the future of CSS may be, so it is imperative that a browser ignore declarations and selectors it doesn't know what to do with. This facilitates advancement of the language (just as it does for HTML) and it also makes it possible to progressively enhance pages using CSS.

For properties, using parsing errors to your advantage is pretty straightforward and it opens up some awesome possibilities. Here's a quick example using CSS3's RGBa color scheme:

```
p {
  background-color: rgb(137, 224, 160);
  background-color: rgba(180, 246, 248, .43);
}
```

A browser parsing this rule set would likely understand the selector (after all, you can't get much simpler than an element selector), so it would move on to the first `background-color` declaration. The `background-color` property has been a part of CSS since version 1, so the browser should have no problem there and would move on to the assigned value. Similarly, RGB-based color values have also been a part of CSS since the beginning, so the browser will understand that value. With the first declaration passing muster with the parser, the browser would apply `background-color: rgb(137, 224, 160);` to all paragraphs and the parser would move on to the second declaration.

In the second declaration, `background-color` is redefined with a new value (per the cascade). Obviously, as we discussed, the browser understands the property, so it would move on to the declared value, which uses RGBa. If the browser understands RGBa, there's no problem and the RGBa value is assigned to the `background-color` property, overwriting the original RGB value. If RGBa is not supported, however, the browser experiences a parsing error and ignores the entire declaration, leaving all paragraphs with an RGB value for `background-color`.

In this example, browsers that comprehend RGBa values would overwrite the `background-color` value following the rules of the "cascade" (as in Cascading Style Sheets). I'll go into the cascade a bit more thoroughly later in the chapter, but here's a quick summary: the cascade dictates that, for equivalent properties, the last one defined is the one rendered.

This is a pretty simple example of how we can use CSS' fault-tolerant nature to deliver an enhanced experience to more capable browsers. It doesn't just work at the declaration level either; you can apply this same technique to hide entire rule sets from a particular browser by using a more advanced selector:

```
html[lang] p {
  /* A bunch of advanced stuff goes here */
}
```

Any browser encountering this rule set would parse it, starting with the selector. If the browser understands attribute-based selection (in this case targeting any paragraph that is a descendant of an `html` element that has a language attribute), it will continue parsing the rule set and apply the declarations it understands. If, on the other hand, said browser does not comprehend attribute selectors, it would experience a parsing error and ignore the entire rule set.

Perhaps the most famous example of using this technique to selectively deliver rules to one browser over another (more for effect than practicality) is Egor Kloos' CSS Zen Garden entry titled "Gemination."[3]

Figure 3.1: *Gemination in IE6 (above) and IE7 (below).*

3. http://www.csszengarden.com/062/

In this proof-of-concept piece, Kloos created a basic layout aimed at Internet Explorer (then in version 6) and employed a technique dubbed MOSe ("Mozilla/Opera/Safari enhancement")[4] to offer more advanced browsers a completely different experience. Kloos used simple selectors for the basic layout and advanced selectors for the enhanced styles. Here's a snippet that demonstrates his approach:

```
#intro {
  margin: 0;
  padding: 0;
  width: 660px;
  height: 80px;
  background: transparent url(introkop.gif)
    no-repeat right top;
}

/* ... */

body[id=css-zen-garden] #intro {
  position: absolute;
  top: 0;
  left: 0;
  float: none;
  margin: 0;
  width: 100%;
  height: 350px;
  background: none;
}
```

Following CSS cascade order, the browser parses the first rule set first to render the #intro layout. A little later, the browser parses the "enhanced" rule set for #intro. If the browser understands attribute selectors, it will render a completely different layout for #intro; if it doesn't, it will ignore the new rule set entirely.

---

4. Dave Shea, curator of the CSS Zen Garden, coined the term back in 2003, but when Internet Explorer 7 came out, the term fell out of use because it didn't have the same selector-based limitations as IE6. You can read his original post at http://www.mezzoblue.com/archives/2003/06/25/mose/

Selector-based screening can be a useful technique, but it tends to trip up many CSS authors who don't realize selector failure in a compound selector (two or more selector statements, separated by commas) is complete and not discrete:

```
p,
p:not([title]) {
  color: red;
  font-style: bold;
}
```

This example has the same five locations for potential parsing errors as the example that opened this chapter, but it also has a sixth one in the second selector (p:not([title])). Browsers that understand only one of these two selectors will ignore *the entire rule set* rather than just the advanced selector (which, in case you were wondering, looks for paragraphs without title attributes).

Though it may seem unintuitive, the CSS 2.1 spec very clearly states that this is how it should be: "The whole statement should be ignored if there is an error anywhere in the selector, even though the rest of the selector may look reasonable."[5] Knowing this, we can make better decisions about how and when to combine selectors. As a general rule, it's best to avoid combining advanced selectors with simple ones (as in the example) unless you *want* to hide the whole rule set from older browsers.

We'll come back to this technique momentarily, but first let's take a quick detour through the world of specificity.

Specificity is another core concept in CSS. It is a measure of how many elements a given selector can select and is the only mechanism available for overruling the cascade (more

---

5. http://www.w3.org/TR/2009/CR-CSS2-20090908/syndata.
    html#rule-sets

on that in a second). Some selectors are more specific than other selectors. For example, an `id` selector (e.g., `#intro`) is 10 times more specific than a `class` selector (e.g., `.vcard`), which is, in turn, 10 times more specific than an element selector (e.g., `p`).[6]

The specificity of a given selector is calculated by adding the specificity of all of its component parts. Rules applied via very specific selectors will trump those applied with less specific selectors, regardless of their order in the cascade. Looking back at Egor's attribute selection sleight-of-hand, it's worth noting that even if the first rule set in the example came second in the CSS file, the browser would still prioritize it lower than the other rule set because its selector has a lower specificity value than that of the second rule set.

Specificity of selectors is something that takes time to master and can cause any number of headaches because if you apply all of your styles with heavy-handed selectors (e.g., each one contains an `id` selector), you end up having to create even more specific selectors to overrule them (e.g., two `id` selectors). To avoid an ever-escalating arms race of specificity, I recommend that you avoid making your selectors unnecessarily specific.

Let's revisit Kloos' handiwork and apply what we learned regarding parsing errors in compound selectors; in doing so, we can reduce the specificity of Egor's advanced rule sets and still maintain the spirit of his original work:

```
#intro {
  /* Old Layout */
}

/* ... */
```

---

6. If you don't quite grasp how specificity is calculated, be sure to check out Andy Clarke's "CSS Specificity Wars" http://www. stuffandnonsense.co.uk/archives/css_specificity_wars. html.

```
[foo], #intro {
  /* Advanced Layout */
}
```

In this revision, I changed the second rule set into a compound selector targeting an element with an attribute named "foo" and another element with an id of "intro." The trick to this approach is that the initial attribute selector is a red herring. The foo attribute is not only non-standard, but it is not used anywhere in the CSS Zen Garden HTML, so the addition of that selector to the rule set does nothing but hide the rule set from browsers that don't understand attribute selectors. And, most importantly, it leaves the #intro selector unadulterated, keeping its specificity equal to that of the previous rule, allowing the cascade to determine style application.

While this may not always be the technique you immediately reach for when implementing CSS, it's a good one to remember when you want to use rule set filtering without altering a selector's specificity. From a maintainability standpoint, this method is not ideal for more than a single rule set here and there; to apply the concept of rule set filtering *en masse*, there are better options available, and we'll get to those shortly.

CONCERNS, SEPARATED

The "cascade" is a critically important concept in CSS; in fact it's the *first word* in CSS. Literally. Again, it's beyond the scope of this little book to go through the concept of the cascade in any detail, but there is one facet that can help you become a progressive enhancement expert in no time: order.

Order matters. A lot.

In CSS, when all else is equal (i.e., specificity), the proximity of a style declaration to its target element determines the

outcome. We saw this in our earlier example with the two
background-color assignments and the same holds true
with independent rule sets.

```
h1 {
  font-size: 2em;
}

h1 {
  font-size: 3em;
}
```

In this case, h1 elements will be assigned a font-size value
of 3em. While it's unlikely you'll see the same selector used
in two consecutive rule sets like this, it's not uncommon to
see something similar. Take, for example, the images in the
"Lodging" article on the Retreats 4 Geeks site:

Where You'll Stay

**This is about as far from industrial carpeting and folding
chairs as you can get.**

Our luxury lodge is located on the side of a mountain in Sevierville,
Tennessee, just outside of Gatlinburg. Equipped with a 4x8 foot
theater screen, wireless internet, a hot tub, a pool table, a dartboard,
a bar, and gorgeous views of the surrounding mountains, it's the
perfect atmosphere to escape the daily grind and learn something
new.

Each of the lodge's twelve suites has a king-sized bed, private
bathroom with a jacuzzi tub, and its own balcony so you can relax and
relish your surroundings. You can even bring a guest for a small
additional fee (see the registration form).

In addition to filling your head with knowledge, we'll fill your tummy with tasty organic meals (and plenty of snacks for when you
get peckish), all prepared in-house by our personal chef. And if you have dietary restrictions or preferences, we'll do everything
we can to accommodate and offer tasty choices.

Looking for a detailed curriculum or more information to help sell your boss on this event? Download the HTML5 & CSS3 fact
sheet or view our frequently asked questions. Ready to attend? Register now.

Figure 3.2: *The Lodging article.*

The underlying markup for this article is as follows:

```
<article id="lodging">

  <header>
   <h1>Where You&#8217;ll Stay</h1>
  </header>

  <figure class="frame focal">
   <img class="inner" src="i/lodge.jpg"
    alt="" title="..."/>
  </figure>

  <section class="main">
   <!-- description of accommodations -->
  </section>

  <aside class="extra">
   <ul class="gallery">
    <li>
     <figure class="frame">
      <img class="inner" src="i/room.jpg"
       alt="" title="..."/>
     </figure>
    </li>
    <!-- ... -->
   </ul>
  </aside>

</article>
```

You'll notice that the article in question uses the same class for each figure element: "frame"; this allows us to achieve consistency with regard to the postcard-with-matte look. I've given the focal figure an additional class of, well, "focal." This setup allows me to use two different CSS rules of equal specificity to apply the appropriate styles to figure. focal. Here's an example of one such application, followed by an override:

```
.frame {
  margin: 0 auto 40px;
}

.focal {
  margin: 0 20px 25px 30px;
}
```

Each of these rule sets applies to the focal figure in this article (and all others on the page) and both rule sets have selectors of equal specificity. Since the second rule set defines the same property as the first, the margin value of the "focal" figure will be "0 20px 25px 30px" instead of "0 auto 40px."

Of course, most stylesheets are composed of hundreds of rule sets, making it easy to unintentionally fall victim to issues of proximity. Thankfully, however, we can alleviate some of those issues by taking a layered approach to designing with CSS.

Taking a step back for a moment, you can see the design of a website contains three core facets: Typography, color, and layout. Each brings something more to the table, building the design until it is fully realized. When it comes to progressive enhancement with CSS, we can use that same breakdown to create discrete levels of support that are delivered based on the capabilities of the browser: typography; typography and color; and typography, color, and layout.

As we've discussed, rule order matters, so when building a progressive design, we must reconcile our desire to separate the facets of our design with the way the cascade prescribes the interpretation of our rules. In practical terms, that means delivering your groups of facet-specific declarations in a set order: typography, then layout, then color. Why that order? We'll get to that in a moment.

You can deliver these rule groups as separate stylesheets (either linked or imported) or in a single one.[7] The multiple stylesheet route is pretty straightforward and easy to manage, but it costs you in performance because each stylesheet must be obtained in a separate HTTP request. Beyond that, some browsers don't cache stylesheets more than one level down (e.g., a stylesheet imported into another stylesheet). For these reasons, the single stylesheet approach makes the most sense to me and is the one I've implemented on the Retreats 4 Geeks site.

To illustrate the concept of layering styles, perhaps it's best to start at the beginning: with no style applied. On the following page, Figure 3.3 shows the lodging article in Safari with only the default browser styles applied.

As you can see, the content is completely usable with the browser's default styles. It's not nearly as attractive as we'd like, but the content is entirely accessible. Applying a layer of general typographic styles, we end up with Figure 3.4.

---

7. Just because your CSS is delivered in one stylesheet doesn't mean it needs to be maintained that way. There are numerous server-side tools for combining CSS files into a single one, so you could easily have the best of both worlds by physically importing the separate stylesheets into the slots in a single skeleton CSS file before delivering it to your users. For an example: http://www.easy-reader.net/archives/2010/07/11/template-based-asset-munging-in-expressionengine.

Where You'll Stay

This is about as far from industrial carpeting and folding chairs as you can get.

Our luxury lodge is located on the side of a mountain in Sevierville, Tennessee, just outside of Gatlinburg. Equipped with a 4x8 foot theater screen, wireless internet, a hot tub, a pool table, a dartboard, a bar, and gorgeous views of the surrounding mountains, it's the perfect atmosphere to escape the daily grind and learn something new.

Each of the lodge's twelve suites has a king-sized bed, private bathroom with a jacuzzi tub, and its own balcony so you can relax and relish your surroundings. You can even bring a guest for a small additional fee (see the registration form).

In addition to filling your head with knowledge, we'll fill your tummy with tasty organic meals (and plenty of snacks for when you get peckish), all prepared in-house by our personal chef. And if you have dietary restrictions or preferences, we'll do everything we can to accommodate and offer tasty choices.

Looking for a detailed curriculum or more information to help sell your boss on this event? Download the HTML5 & CSS3 fact sheet or view our frequently asked questions. Ready to attend? Register now.

Figure 3.3: *"Lodging" sans CSS.*

Where You'll Stay

This is about as far from industrial carpeting and folding chairs as you can get.

Our luxury lodge is located on the side of a mountain in Sevierville, Tennessee, just outside of Gatlinburg. Equipped with a 4x8 foot theater screen, wireless internet, a hot tub, a pool table, a dartboard, a bar, and gorgeous views of the surrounding mountains, it's the perfect atmosphere to escape the daily grind and learn something new.

Each of the lodge's twelve suites has a king-sized bed, private bathroom with a jacuzzi tub, and its own balcony so you can relax and relish your surroundings. You can even bring a guest for a small additional fee (see the registration form).

In addition to filling your head with knowledge, we'll fill your tummy with tasty organic meals (and plenty of snacks for when you get peckish), all prepared in-house by our personal chef. And if you have dietary restrictions or preferences, we'll do everything we can to accommodate and offer tasty choices.

Looking for a detailed curriculum or more information to help sell your boss on this event? Download the HTML5 & CSS3 fact sheet or view our frequently asked questions. Ready to attend? Register now.

Figure 3.4: *"Lodging" with typographic styles.*

The improvement is minor, but it is an improvement. And for browsers that have issues with CSS-based layouts, this may actually serve your users better than trying to force them into a more advanced layout than their browser can handle.

The next layer of style support to offer—and one that's probably available to users alongside basic typography— is color (which, in some cases, may include background images). Figure 3.5 shows the minor changes color brings to the design of this article.

Where You'll Stay

This is about as far from industrial carpeting and folding chairs as you can get.

Our luxury lodge is located on the side of a mountain in Sevierville, Tennessee, just outside of Gatlinburg. Equipped with a 4x8 foot theater screen, wireless internet, a hot tub, a pool table, a dartboard, a bar, and gorgeous views of the surrounding mountains, it's the perfect atmosphere to escape the daily grind and learn something new.

Each of the lodge's twelve suites has a king-sized bed, private bathroom with a jacuzzi tub, and its own balcony so you can relax and relish your surroundings. You can even bring a guest for a small additional fee (see the registration form).

In addition to filling your head with knowledge, we'll fill your tummy with tasty organic meals (and plenty of snacks for when you get peckish), all prepared in-house by our personal chef. And if you have dietary restrictions or preferences, we'll do everything we can to accommodate and offer tasty choices.

Looking for a detailed curriculum or more information to help sell your boss on this event? Download the HTML5 & CSS3 fact sheet or view our frequently asked questions. **Ready to attend?** Register now.

Figure 3.5: *"Lodging," colorized.*

Clearly, we're looking at incremental improvements here, but improvements nonetheless.

The final layer of style application we'll concern ourselves with right now is the screen-based layout. Figure 3.2, from earlier in the chapter, shows the "Lodging" article in all of its glory.

You may recall that I mentioned I've chosen to define all of these layers in a single file. To accomplish that, I broke the file down into three distinct sections as seen in this excerpt highlighting the styles applied to the images of the "Lodging" article:

```css
/* =Typography */
img {
  display:block;
}

/* =Layout */
@media screen {
  .frame .inner {
    border: 10px solid;
  }
}

/* =Color */
.frame .inner {
  background-color: rgb(227, 222, 215);
  border-color: rgb(227, 222, 215);
}
```

You were probably quick to notice the @media block that contains layout rules for the screen. The use of @media here is not accidental: it ensures that every medium is given access to the typography and color rules while the layout rules are restricted to user agents that implement the "screen" media type. Following this setup, you can easily do the same for print or any other medium, but more on that in a bit.

The use of @media has another benefit as well: really old browsers (e.g., Netscape 4) don't understand it. And, following the rules of fault tolerance, browsers ignore anything they don't understand, so our layout styles remain cleverly hidden from older browsers and devices, leaving them with a purely typographic or, as is more likely, a colorful typographic experience.

Now, getting back to an earlier question, why are the color rules last? Well, my reasoning is simple: I like CSS shorthand. CSS shorthand allows us to combine multiple declarations into a single one. We saw an example of CSS shorthand earlier: `border: 10px solid`. This declaration is shorthand for:

```
border-top: 10px solid;
border-right: 10px solid;
border-bottom: 10px solid;
border-left: 10px solid;
```

Incidentally, each of those declarations is also shorthand. For example, `border-top: 10px solid` is shorthand for:

```
border-top-width: 10px;
border-top-style: solid;
border-top-color: inherit;
```

As you can see, CSS shorthand greatly reduces the complexity of your stylesheets.

Glancing back at the previous example, imagine that the color rule set had been moved before the layout one. The `border-color` would be set to a light gray. Then, in the layout rules, the `border` shorthand is used, overwriting the `border-color` declaration from the earlier rule. It does this because the specificity of the rule sets is identical and the `border` shorthand always sets the `border-color`, even if you don't explicitly define it ("inherit" is the default value, meaning it uses the text color). That's why I recommend defining color rules last. Shorthand can be really useful for simplifying and compressing your stylesheets, but you need to be aware of the order in which you apply them.

Since we're on the topic of color, I'll also mention that in certain cases, you may want to use color in a layout-specific context (e.g., a background color). In those instances, it may make sense to block out a subsection of your rules using `@media`, just as we did with the overall layout:

```
/* =Color */
.frame .inner {
  /* colors for every medium */
}

@media screen {
  .frame .inner {
    /* screen-only colors */
  }
}
```

With our faceted framework in place, it becomes quite simple to introduce additional modules as the need arises. For example, effects:

```
/* =Color */
a:link, a:visited {
  color: rgb(180, 49, 25);
}

a:hover {
  color: rgb(235, 123, 35);
}
/* ... */

/* =Effects */
@media screen {
  a {
    transition-duration: .5s;
  }
}
```

Now that you have a pretty solid understanding of how to wield CSS's inherent fault tolerance for the betterment of the browsing experience, let's delve a little deeper and layer on some additional enhancements.

A LITTLE MISUNDERSTANDING GOES A LONG WAY

As a fault-tolerant language, CSS is a near perfect addition to the progressive enhancement toolbox. In many ways, ignorance is bliss because we can reliably use new features and syntax without having to worry about the browser falling apart when it doesn't understand something. But what if a browser *thinks* it understands something, but its understanding is horribly flawed? Yes, of course, I'm speaking of Internet Explorer.

IE9 was released as this book was in production. Based on what I've seen so far, it looks like the team has made good on their promise to support standards (including CSS) in a completely interoperable way. IE8 was no slouch in the CSS department, but when you start looking back at IE7 and (shudder) IE6, things take a turn for the worse.

Thankfully, the smart folks at Microsoft gave us a tool that makes it easy to sequester browser-specific patches to CSS, JavaScript, and even markup: Conditional Comments.[8] Conditional Comments are exactly what you'd expect: a specifically-formatted HTML comment that is interpreted by IE but is ignored by all other browsers (because it's a comment).

Conditional Comments are a boon for the progressive enhancement world because, while progressive enhancement isn't really about the browser, in practical application, some browsers need a little hand-holding to meet the needs of our users. Conditional Comments give us authors the ability to target a specific version (or versions) of IE. Here's a quick example of how to put them to use:

---

8.   http://msdn.microsoft.com/en-us/library/
      ms537512(VS.85).aspx

```
<link rel="stylesheet" href="c/main.css"/>
<!--[if IE 9]><link rel="stylesheet"
  href="c/ie9.css"/><![endif]-->
<!--[if lte IE 8]><link rel="stylesheet"
  href="c/ie8.css"/><![endif]-->
<!--[if lte IE 7]><link rel="stylesheet"
  href="c/ie7.css"/><![endif]-->
<!--[if lte IE 6]><link rel="stylesheet"
  href="c/ie6.css"/><![endif]-->
```

In this particular snippet, you can see that we are including our core CSS file (`main.css`) on the first line. After that, we have a conditionally-commented stylesheet directed at IE9, using the syntax `if IE 9`. Skip that one for a moment and focus on the following three lines, the first of which targets IE8 and below (`if lte IE 8` {meaning "if less than or equal to IE8"}), the second of which targets IE7 and below (`if lte IE 7`), and the final line which targets IE6 and below. Used in concert and in this specific order, these three conditionally-commented stylesheets streamline the CSS patching process by allowing the patches you applied to more recent versions of IE to trickle down to earlier versions. The reasoning? Well, if an issue exists in IE7, it's pretty likely that IE6 had the same problem.

The conditional comment for IE9, by contrast, only targets that specific browser. It could easily be set up in the same "less than or equal to" manner as the subsequent conditional comments, but IE9 is a substantial departure from IE8 on many levels, including its CSS support. Any issues it has are not likely to be issues with those earlier browsers, so there's no need to make those older browsers read and parse the additional rules. The same setup could have been done for IE8 as well, as the mechanisms that define its CSS support are completely different than those in IE7 and it shares few, if any, issues with IE7 and earlier, but as the design requires that we use some IE-specific filters, it made sense to only have to write them once.

BEYOND THE BASICS

The web is unlike any other medium we've encountered thus far. It isn't print, television, radio, a video game, a kiosk, or an application, but it functions as a hybrid of all of these things and more. Realizing this, the W3C added the ability to target styles to a specific medium. We took advantage of that capability earlier in an @media block, but you're probably more familiar with using media declarations with linked or embedded stylesheets (using the media attribute) or, possibly, as a suffix to @import statements.

The W3C maintains the list of approved media types, but is open to adding to it as technology evolves. Currently, the list addresses CSS' application on the computer screen, in print, on televisions, on hand held devices, and in assistant contexts such as screen readers, braille printers, and touch feedback devices. Without a specific media designation, the browser assumes a media type of "screen."

At their most basic, media assignments use a single media designation, but as with selectors, multiple media assignments can be combined using a comma (which acts as an implicit "or"). In the following example, main.css would be applied for both "print" and "screen" media types:

```
<link rel="stylesheet" href="main.css"
  media="screen, print"/>
```

Media assignments are fault tolerant, though the application of fault tolerance for media assignments is quite different from what is applied to selectors (not that that's confusing at all): if unknown media types in a comma-separated series are encountered, *they are simply ignored* and the known media types remain honored.[9]

Unfortunately, in the case of media declarations on @import, IE versions prior to 8 spoil the party even when the media type is one they understand. Yet another reason it's best to stick with @media, unless you specifically want to hide certain rules from that browser:

```
@import 'not-for-IE7-or-below.css' screen;
@media screen, print, refrigerator {
  /* IE will get these rules */
}
```

Media assignments are incredibly powerful because they allow us to create layouts that adapt to the medium in which they are presented. One of the first applications of this technique came from Eric Meyer in 2000, when he showed us how to jettison "printer friendly" pages and use a media-specific stylesheet to provide a printer-friendly view of any web page.[10] Two years later, he built on that concept and showed us how we could use advanced CSS (such as generated content) to progressively enhance that same experience.[11]

Returning to our main stylesheet, we can add support for alternate media within our faceted framework quite easily:

---

9. The CSS 2.1 spec (http://www.w3.org/TR/2009/CR-CSS2-20090908/media.html#media-types) addresses this explicitly in the case of @media and @import, but is oddly non-prescriptive about the same behavior applying to linked and embedded styles. Still, all modern browsers treat the HTML-based media designations the same way.

10. http://meyerweb.com/eric/articles/webrev/200001.html

11. http://www.alistapart.com/articles/goingtoprint/

```
/* =Typography */
/* typography for every medium */
@media screen {
  /* screen-only typography */
}
@media print {
  /* print-only typography */
}

/* =Layout */
/* layout for every medium */
@media screen {
  /* screen-only layout */
}
@media print {
  /* print-only layout */
}

/* =Color */
/* colors for every medium */
@media screen {
  /* screen-only colors */
}
@media print {
  /* print-only colors */
}
```

Or all of the styles for print could be bundled into a single @media declaration at the bottom:

```
/* =Typography */
/* typography for every medium */
@media screen {
  /* screen-only typography */
}

/* =Layout */
/* layout for every medium */
@media screen {
  /* screen-only layout */
}
```

```
/* =Color */
/* colors for every medium */
@media screen {
  /* screen-only colors */
}

/* =Print */
@media print {
  /* global print-only overrides */
}
```

In the case of print, it may make the most sense to have a single @media declaration to handle everything, but with other media, it may be advisable to break it up. Each project is different, so you'll want to play around and see what feels right.

Not your father's media declarations

A few years after the introduction of independent media support, the W3C upped the ante even more and introduced media queries. Media queries are like media designations on steroids: they provide details about the user's environment, such as the width of the browser window or even its orientation (as in portrait or landscape). Media queries are incredibly powerful and allow you to really fine-tune your designs for specific devices. As such, they are quickly becoming an indispensable tool in progressive enhancement.

Using media queries (which can go wherever you'd place a standard media designation), you can add a set of rules to a page based on the capabilities of the user agent. Let's take a look at an example:

```
@media (min-width:1025px) {
  /* ... */
}
```

In this case, we designated a group of rule sets to be used only if the browser width is 1025px or more.

The CSS3 module that defines media queries reached the Candidate Recommendation stage in the middle of 2009 and prescribes how to obtain browser dimensions as well as numerous other aspects of the device it is running on, such as its dimensions, orientation, color capabilities, resolution, and the like. Not all of the properties are currently supported, but enough are to make them worth considering.

Media queries build upon the standard media designation syntax by introducing the "and" combinator and negation using the "not" keyword. These additions give you a bit more flexibility to target the screen medium where the browser is over 1024px wide (`screen and (min-width:1025px)`), or anything besides print (`not print`), but they do not add an explicit "or," so you can't perform more complicated queries like you can in an actual programming language (e.g., A and B or B and C, but not A and C). You can, however, imply "or" using a comma.

Here's a rather exhaustive compound media query with an explanation of what it does in the comment:

```
@media
  screen and (min-device-width:1024px) and
  (max-width:989px),
  screen and (max-device-width:480px),
  screen and (max-device-width:480px) and
  (orientation:landscape),
  screen and (min-device-width:481px) and
  (orientation:portrait) {
  /* Layout for narrower desktop browser window
     (below 990px) or
     iPhone running iOS 3 (or equivalent) or
     iPhone running iOS 4 (or equivalent) in
     "landscape" view or
     iPad (or equivalent) in "portrait" view */
}
```

Revisiting our example stylesheet, I have used media queries to progressively enhance the page by making a baseline layout aimed at older browsers and tablets. I then adjust the layout for wider desktop browsers and narrower smartphones:

```
/* =Basic Layout */
@media screen {
  /* ... */
}

/* =Full Layout */
@media screen and (min-width:1025px) {
  /* ... */
}

/* =Narrow Layout  */
@media screen and (max-width:765px) {
  /* ... */
}
```

Figure 3.6 shows the alternate layouts available. In some instances the changes from version to version are pretty drastic (e.g., each has a different navigation treatment) while others are more subtle (e.g., the postcard-based contact form adjusts to accommodate a narrower screen). Without getting caught up in the specific differences between these layouts, the important thing to recognize is that media queries can be used to create truly adaptive layouts using only CSS. For more information on adaptive layouts, consult the "Further Reading" section of Chapter 6.

NARROW

REGULAR/TABLET

```
@media screen and
    (max-width:765px) {
    /* ... */
}
```

```
@media screen {
    /* ... */
}
```

WIDE

```
@media screen and (min-width:1025px) {
    /* ... */
}
```

Figure 3.6: *Alternate layouts with media queries.*

RICH IN LAYERS

As you can see, there are numerous ways we can use CSS to progressively enhance our web pages. Some techniques, such as taking advantage of parsing errors, are so simple and commonplace that you're probably using them right now. Others, such as faceted style separation, may provide a slightly different take on your current practices or may be completely foreign to you. When used in combination, however, these techniques weave together, layer upon layer, to provide a tailored experience for every user, no matter what her browser or device supports.

"I don't want to use a tool unless I'm going to use it really well. Doing any of these things halfway is worse than not at all. People don't want a mediocre interaction."

— SETH GODIN

CHAPTER 4:
PROGRESSIVE ENHANCEMENT WITH JAVASCRIPT

On February 7th, 2011, shortly after Gawker Media launched a unified redesign of their various blogs (Lifehacker, Gizmodo, etc.), users visiting any of those sites were greeted by a blank stare (see Figure 4.1). The new platform relied entirely on JavaScript to load content into the page and an error in that JavaScript code made any page request come up empty-handed.[1] That single error caused a lengthy "site outage" (I use that term liberally because the servers were still working) for every Gawker property and lost them countless page views and ad impressions. And it could have been avoided, had they designed their new platform using progressive enhancement.

---

1. A brief mention of the outage is here: http://blogs.wsj.com/digits/2011/02/07/gawker-outage-causing-twitter-stir/. Jeremy Keith and Mike Isolani provided worthwhile commentary on the JavaScript reliance of Gawker's platform (http://adactio.com/journal/4346/ and http://isolani.co.uk/blog/javascript/BreakingTheWebWithHashBangs, respectively). I also weighed in at http://easy-reader.net/archives/2011/02/09/you-cant-rely-on-javascript/.

Figure 4.1: *Lifehacker. Empty.*

Nothing really makes a web page sing quite like JavaScript. With it, you can create rich interactions, build dynamic interfaces, and so on. Web developers realized this early on. They jumped at the opportunity to wield this powerful tool to build more engaging web pages, validate form data, and more. For today's JavaScript developers, it's easy to make something amazing and stick to the progressive enhancement philosophy, but it wasn't always that way.

Back in the mid-to-late '90s, coding JavaScript was like practicing a dark art. For every bit of spaghetti code we had in our HTML, it was usually ten times worse in JavaScript because the two dominant browsers at the time, Netscape and Internet Explorer, each had their own implementation of the language[2] and they differed just enough to make the really interesting stuff incredibly gnarly to write. For example, finding the same element (e.g., #location) in the document (technically the Document Object Model or DOM) required two incredibly different syntaxes:

```
document.layers['location'];  // Netscape
document.all['location'];     // IE
```

---

2. The JavaScript language itself, designed by Brendan Eich, debuted as a feature of Netscape 2 in late 1995. Microsoft developed its own dialect of JavaScript (named "JScript," for trademark reasons) and released it in mid 1996 as part of Internet Explorer 3 (which was, coincidentally, also the first browser to offer CSS support).

This unfortunate reality required us to essentially write every script twice, or at least fill it with "forks" (alternate paths for a script to take, based on the browser) that came back to "fork" us in the end.

As we discussed in Chapter 2, the late '90s was a period of great turmoil on the web: the browser wars. With each new release, Netscape and Microsoft offered up new goodies for developers to use, hoping to capture a greater share of the browser market. This one-upmanship created a lot of problems for developers; with the two competing implementations of JavaScript, we spent so much time trying to even out the discrepancies that we didn't pay attention to how the language functioned or learn the best way to integrate it with HTML and CSS.

When the European Computer Manufacturers Association (ECMA) International standardized JavaScript[3] and the W3C released its DOM spec, the shifting sands beneath our feet were finally replaced with a solid foundation and we were able to start figuring out better ways of doing things:

```
document.getElementById('location'); // Unified DOM
```

GETTING OUT OF THE WAY

One of the first lessons we learned when the dust settled was that JavaScript was not a panacea for interaction on the web. In fact, it wasn't even all that reliable.

First off, even after the W3C standardized the DOM and the browsers generally agreed to support web standards, not everyone was reading from the same playbook; there

---

3. Netscape submitted JavaScript to ECMA International for consideration as a standard in 1996. The standardized version of Javascript became known as "ECMAScript," but we generally use JavaScript unless referring to a spec.

were enough differences between implementations that it was simply impossible to make any assumptions about the availability of certain methods (such as the lynchpin DOM traversal methods `document.getElementById()`, which provides access to elements based on their `id` or `document.getElementsByTagName()` which, you guessed it, finds elements based on their name). Secondly, even if a browser did have full JavaScript support, the user (or her IT administrator) still had the final say over whether or not JavaScript was even allowed to run.[4]

Over time, we realized that JavaScript support was not a given and we began to re-factor our code, making it cleaner, more maintainable, and more flexible to deal with the availability (or absence) of JavaScript. Let's examine the thinking during that period to better understand how to use JavaScript progressively.

Warning: From here on out, we'll be diving into actual JavaScript code. If you have not worked much with JavaScript before, have no fear, I'll do my best to explain what's happening at every step of the way so that you can follow along, even if the code reads like Sanskrit to you.

100% reliance

Back in the early days of JavaScript, it was not uncommon to write (or at least see) onclick event handlers (scripts executed

---

4. For IT administrators, however, the choice to disable Javascript was fundamentally a security one, but for a long time users with accessibility concerns were also encouraged to disable JavaScript. Some users also disabled JavaScript to remove annoying ads and popups. JavaScript is most easily disabled in the browser preferences, but can also be blocked by firewalls or disabled at the application level by IT administrators.

when someone clicked an element on the page) adorning otherwise useless links.[5]

```
<a href="#" onclick="newWin( 'http://easy-designs.
  net/' );">Easy! Designs</a>
```

With JavaScript enabled, this link calls a custom function named newWin, passing it a value of "http://easy-designs. net/." That function, in turn, opens that URL in a new window. Without JavaScript, however, the link wouldn't do anything because, as you'll recall from our discussion of identifiers in Chapter 2, the href points to an empty id. What's the point of a link that won't work without JavaScript?

Which brings me to my first maxim for progressive enhancement with JavaScript:

1. Make sure all content is accessible and all necessary tasks can be completed without JavaScript turned on.

This link obviously violates that (as does the Gawker platform I mentioned earlier), but so did the vast majority of JavaScript in use on the web by the end of the '90s. At that time, the web was lousy with sites that required JavaScript and places where it got in the way of users; in other words, where JavaScript was obtrusive. Realizing this problem, web developers began to push for "unobtrusive" JavaScript.

Note: I'm not advocating the use of popups or using JavaScript to open new windows as they introduce a number of accessibility and usability issues. I have, however, chosen this as an example because it illustrates the evolution of our JavaScript code in a manner that's relatively easy to follow. Rest assured, the lessons

---

5. Variations of this old school technique included the javascript pseudo-protocol (e.g., <a href="javascript:myFuncti on();">) and, my personal favorite, the combined use of the javascript pseudo-protocol and an inline event handler (e.g., <a href="javascript:void(null)" onclick="myFunction();">).

you'll learn by following this example are universally applicable to any other JavaScript-ing you might do.

Becoming unobtrusive

Unobtrusive JavaScript is a catch-all term for programming in a manner that is not reliant on JavaScript. Under this paradigm, users are given access to all page content and can accomplish every necessary task on a page using the basic building blocks of the web (HTML and the HTTP protocol). JavaScript is then layered on to enhance the page.

Sound familiar? Unobtrusive JavaScript is an idea that meshes perfectly with progressive enhancement philosophy because it forces JavaScript into the role of functional enhancement, as opposed to absolute requirement.

With unobtrusive JavaScript in mind, we re-factored our links to work whether JavaScript was available or not:

```
<a href="http://easy-designs.net/" onclick="newWin
  ( this.href ); return false;">Easy! Designs</a>
```

In this revision, the link actually points to a URL so it will function without JavaScript. When JavaScript is available, however, clicking the link will call newWin, which is passed the value of the link's href attribute (the DOM value this.href). The other key difference between this and the previous version of the link is that the onclick event handler is also set to "return false," which cancels the click event's default action (in this case, following the link to a new page).

This was a great first step to address the potential absence of JavaScript, but we soon realized there were better ways to manage scenarios like this.

More maintainable

The next step in the evolution of this code involved using the age-old rel attribute (which you'll recall from Chapter 2) to migrate our inline JavaScript code to an external file. This provided two benefits: 1) it gave an additional semantic meaning to the link and 2) it made maintaining websites much easier because developers could change a single JavaScript file and affect the entire site (which is the exact argument we made for external stylesheets over inline use of the style attribute). Here's the new HTML:

```
<a rel="external" href="http://easy-designs.net/">
  Easy! Designs</a>
```

From there, it's fairly simple to apply the click event to this and any other "external" links:

```
var links = document.getElementsByTagName( 'a' ),
    rel, i = links.length;
while ( i-- ) {
  rel = links[i].getAttribute('rel');
  if ( rel && rel.match( /\bexternal\b/ ) ) {
    links[i].onclick = function(){
      newWin( this.href );
      return false;
    };
  }
}
```

If all those "ifs" and "whiles" are Greek to you, here's a quick summary of what the script does: it collects all of the links on the page and loops through them (in reverse order which, oddly enough, is a bit faster than going forward); and if the link has a rel attribute and its value contains the text "external," the link's onclick event is assigned an anonymous function that calls a function named newWin (passing it the value of the link's href attribute just like in the previous example) before canceling the click's default action by returning false.

Finally, we'd come upon a decent solution that was just about as unobtrusive as you could get and, in 2006, Jeremy Keith gave us a lovely little name for it: Hijax, a clever combination of "hijack," referring to the fact that the link's normal behavior was being commandeered, and Ajax, the JavaScript-based mechanism by which web pages could interact with a server without requiring a refresh in the browser. Little did we know, Ajax, which was just growing in popularity at the time, would show us we still had a thing or two to learn when it came to JavaScript event management.

Truly flexible

With the widespread acceptance and implementation of Ajax techniques[6] and other methods of modifying page content on the fly, our age-old method of assigning event handlers wasn't holding up all that well. After all, if new content was injected into the page with a link marked `rel="external"`, it wouldn't have our custom function assigned as an `onclick` event handler. This is because our script was likely run when the page loaded (`window.onload()`) prior to the new link being injected via Ajax.

This presented a tough problem to be sure. In this scenario, it was possible that two links that should act the same would actually act in completely different ways. Can you say usability issue?

---

6. `XMLHttpRequest` is the technology that we use to make requests to the server to send and receive information without requiring the browser to refresh or reload the page. It was invented at Microsoft for Outlook Web Access and debuted in IE5, but it has been adopted by every other browser and is currently being standardized at the W3C. `XMLHttpRequest` is the backbone of Ajax (Asynchronous JavaScript and XML), but despite its namesake, it can communicate by means other than XML. The "A" in Ajax stands for "asynchronous" because this means of communication doesn't require the user to wait for the response; she can continue interacting with the page while the script loads more information from the server.

To address this issue, some folks re-executed the script whenever an Ajax-based HTML injection was completed. It seemed like a good idea, but calling the same function over and over again slowed the browser down considerably because it had to traverse all of the links on the page each and every time.

Then Christian Heilmann reminded us that any event triggered on a particular element actually traverses the DOM tree from the root node (html) to that element and back again in the event capturing and bubbling phases, respectively.[7] That means the "click" event on a link is actually executed on every element between the root node and the link itself... twice[8] (see Figure 4.2). Listening for the event on an element further up the DOM tree is not only more efficient (because you could assign a single event handler rather than hundreds), but it made it possible to trigger actions on dynamic content, thereby helping us overcome the potential usability issue where similar links behaved differently.

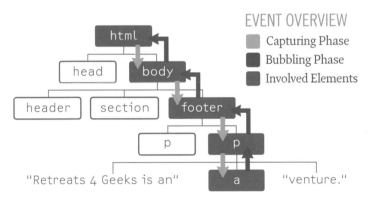

Figure 4.2: *Event capturing and bubbling.*

---

7. http://icant.co.uk/sandbox/eventdelegation/

8. Ok, not technically twice in every browser. The Microsoft event model, the one implemented in all versions of IE prior to 9, only supports the bubbling phase of an event. The standard W3C event model supports both event capturing and event bubbling.

This concept became known as "event delegation" because a single event handler could interpret events and send out orders based on the element that triggered that event. Here's a concise rewrite of the previous example that uses event delegation:

```
document.body.onclick = function( e ) {
  // even out the event models
  e = ( e ) ? e : event;
  var el = e.target || e.srcElement, rel;
  // external links
  rel = el.getAttribute( 'rel' );
  if ( el.nodeName.toLowerCase() == 'a' &&
       rel && rel.match( /\bexternal\b/ ) ) {
    newWin( el.href );
    // cancel the default action
    if (e.preventDefault) {
      e.preventDefault();
    } else {
      e.returnValue = false;
    }
  }
};
```

This code block assigns an event handler to the onclick event of the body element, establishing the listener; within the listener, it determines the target element (the one that was clicked) and then checks to make sure it's an anchor element (a) that has a rel attribute containing the string "external"; if the element meets all of those requirements, the newWin function is called and the event's default action is canceled.

This example, while specific, demonstrates why we must continue to evolve our approach to JavaScript-based interactions. Improving our JavaScript comprehension provides direct benefits for progressive enhancement by helping us make our code smarter and more unobtrusive, but it also helps us in terms of maintainability and performance.

MAKING WHAT WE NEED

By now you're probably getting the gist of unobtrusive JavaScript, but we've only been looking at the user experience from the document side of things. There are numerous ways in which JavaScript-based interactions are far superior to those without it. Client-side form validation, for instance, provides the opportunity to give users immediate feedback on potential errors without requiring that they submit the form first.

Full name   Joe Bloggs   ✔ ok

    Your full name will appear on your public profile

Username | joebloggs | ⇨ ⊕ checking availability...

    Your public profile: http://twitter.com/ **joebloggs**

Password

Full name   Joe Bloggs   ✔ ok

    Your full name will appear on your public profile

Username | joebloggs | username has already been taken

    Your public profile: http://twitter.com/ **joebloggs**

Password

Figure 4.3: *Checking username availability on Twitter.com.*

As we've seen, we need to be careful to make sure that every interface can work without JavaScript, but what about when JavaScript needs additional markup to achieve its goals? Well, that brings us to my second maxim for progressive enhancement with JavaScript:

2. Use JavaScript to generate any additional markup it needs.

JavaScript is really good at generating and modifying markup on the fly. So when you need to enhance an interface with

JavaScript, start with a baseline of semantic, usable markup and baseline styles. Then instruct the script to make necessary HTML and CSS changes required by the new interface once it has determined that it can run without encountering errors.

For an example of this in action, let's return to the Retreats 4 Geeks page.

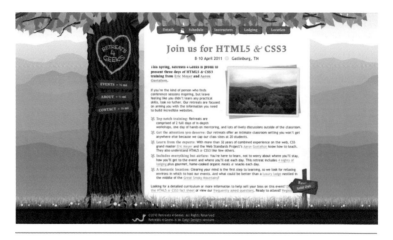

Figure 4.4: *The Retreats 4 Geeks web page.*

I wanted to make the best possible use of space on a mobile device. The horizontal navigation will work on a small browser, but the target areas would be too small to click easily. Of course, I could switch the site to use vertical navigation, allowing for larger links, but that would take up precious screen real estate.

An alternative to these two approaches is creating a dropdown using either CSS or a `select` element. While the pure CSS dropdown option is tempting, the latter approach has an edge because it provides users with a familiar user interface. For that reason, I chose the `select` route.

Based on the markup introduced back in Chapter 2, I'll walk you through creating a script that converts the contents of the nav element into a select when the browser shrinks below a particular size. To keep the example short and a little easier to follow, I've used the jQuery JavaScript library.[9] Libraries are great tools as they are composed of dozens if not hundreds of functions that solve common problems (like adding and removing classes). Don't worry if you can't completely follow the code, I'll explain what's happening so you don't have to decipher it on your own.

We'll begin by isolating the script in an anonymous function[10] that runs as soon as the DOM is available, but before assets like images, CSS files, and videos have been downloaded (a.k.a. onDOMReady). This makes the page more responsive than running a script when the window loads (a.k.a. window. onload). For the remainder of this example, all of the code will be sequestered within this function:

```
$(function(){
  // Exciting stuff will go here
});
```

Next, we create the variables we need for this script to work. By instantiating them all at once, we'll reduce the number of var statements (which helps with minification).[11]

```
var
$window  = $(window),         // reference the window
$old_nav = $('#top nav > *'), // get the navigation
$links   = $old_nav.find('a'),// get the links
showing  = 'old',             // track what's showing
trigger  = 765,               // the browser width
                              // that triggers the change

$new_nav, $option,            // we'll use these shortly
timer    = null;              // we'll need a timer too
```

---

9. http://jQuery.com

10. Anonymous functions are functions which have not been given a name.

11. http://www.alistapart.com/articles/javascript-minification-part-II/

The comments should give you a good sense of what each variable is for.

If you're familiar with jQuery, but confused as to why we're assigning elements to local variables rather than just referencing the jQuery-based lookup (e.g., `$('#top nav > *')`) each time we need it, rest assured that there's a method to my madness: creating a local reference reduces the performance hit of running the script because the look up only happens once instead of every time `$()` is used. Also, to make it easy to differentiate jQuery results from other variables, I've prefaced each associated variable name with a dollar sign ($). You'll see these techniques used throughout this script as they are helpful habits to get into.

With all of our variables in place, you *might* think we could move on to the meat of the script, but we're not quite ready for that yet. Before we try to execute code against the page, we should make sure that the elements we need actually exist:

```
if ( $old_nav.length && $links.length ) {
  // We know the DOM elements we need exist
  // and can do something with them
}
```

Testing for dependencies is very important and is something I'll cover more thoroughly in the next section. Now for the meat (or nutmeat if you're a vegetarian). We'll begin our script in earnest by generating the new `select`-based navigation, creating the `select`, and the first of several `option` elements it will contain:

```
$new_nav = $('<select></select>');
$option = $('<option>-- Navigation --</option>')
  .appendTo($new_nav);
```

With new markup to work with, we can now loop through the links we collected (as `$links`) and build a new option for each by repeatedly cloning the `option` we just created:

```
$links.each(function(){
  var $a = $(this);
  $option.clone()
    .attr( 'value', $a.attr('href') )
    .text( $a.text() )
    .appendTo( $new_nav );
});
```

With the `options` created and appended to the `select` we can move on to adding the final markup touches and setting up the event handler for the `select`'s `onchange` event:

```
$new_nav = $new_nav
  .wrap('<div id="mobile-nav"/>')
  .parent()
  .delegate('select', 'change', function(){
    window.location = $(this).val();
  });
```

This is a slightly simplified version of what you'll find on the live Retreats 4 Geeks site (I've taken out some of the URL hash trickery), but I wanted to make sure you were able to follow it without distraction. Here's what's going on: the first three lines wrap our `select` (`$new_nav`) in a `div` and then re-assign that `div` to the variable `$new_nav` so the whole thing is viewed by JavaScript as a neat little package; the next line uses event delegation (which we discussed earlier) to observe the `onchange` event on the `select` from further up the DOM tree (from the `div`, in fact), assigning an anonymous function to that event that pushes a new location to the browser's address bar (causing the browser to jump to the new section or load a new page, depending on the link type).

Boom! Functional `select`-based navigation. Now to get it into the page when conditions are right. For that, we'll create a new function, called `toggleDisplay`, that will observe the size of the browser window and handle swapping one navigation style for another:

```
function toggleDisplay() {
  var width = $window.width();
  if ( showing == 'old' && width <= trigger ) {
    $old_nav.replaceWith($new_nav);
    showing = 'new';
  } else if ( showing == 'new' && width > trigger ) {
    $new_nav.replaceWith($old_nav);
    showing = 'old';
  }
}
```

Again, this is a slightly simplified version of the final script, but it highlights the important part: the navigation is only swapped in the event that the appropriate browser width threshold is met (trigger) *and* the other navigation style is showing (tracked using showing). With that function in place, we just need to run it once (to initialize everything and make sure the right navigation is showing from the get-go) and then assign it to the window's onresize event:

```
toggleDisplay(); // initialize the right view
$window.resize(function(){
  if ( timer ) { clearTimeout(timer); }
  timer = setTimeout( toggleDisplay, 100 );
});
```

If you're wondering why toggleDisplay() isn't passed in as the actual event handler, that's because doing so would cause the function to be executed numerous times (possibly several hundred) while a user is resizing his or her browser. To keep the number of executions to a minimum (and reduce the burden the script places on a user's CPU), the event handler uses a timer to call toggleDisplay() after .1 seconds. As the function is triggered repeatedly during a resize event, it destroys the timer if it exists and then recreates it. This setup ensures toggleDisplay() is only called once when a user resizes his or her browser (unless he or she does so *very* slowly).

And there you have it: a perfect example of progressive enhancement with JavaScript.

Figure 4.5: select-*based navigation on an iPhone.*

As this simple example demonstrates, JavaScript is perfectly capable of generating everything it needs and getting rid of anything it doesn't. You could even take this particular function a step farther and make it even more markup agnostic by allowing the root starting point (in our case, the child elements of nav) to be passed dynamically into the function. But I leave that to you to experiment with. Onward!

KEEP IT COPACETIC

As we've covered, many of the progressive enhancement techniques available to us in HTML and CSS are pretty straightforward and may even have been part of your repertoire prior to picking up this book. Progressive enhancement with JavaScript, on the other hand, is a bit more complicated; JavaScript cannot be fault tolerant like the others because it is a programming language.

Unlike HTML and CSS, which describe content and provide design instructions to a browser, respectively, JavaScript literally executes commands to the browser. Because they actually *do* something, JavaScript programs stop running when they encounter an error. The potential causes for these errors could be anything from a typo to a missing dependency to accidentally writing an infinite loop. Regardless of the cause, if you write code that doesn't jive well with the browser's JavaScript interpreter, it will likely spit a big fat error right in your face (or your customer's). And no one wants that.

As we've seen, the implementation of progressive enhancement at each stage in the continuum isn't a binary choice of having a particular technology or not having it. Instead, a user's experience at each level is variable based on the capabilities of the browser. So, if a user's browser supports RGBa natively, but not rounded corners, it's not a big deal; the user gets what she gets.

We need to approach JavaScript the same way; it shouldn't be an all or nothing option. Not to keep returning to food metaphors time and time again, but we should offer technologies in an *à la carte* fashion by dividing up the functionality into discrete, self-contained packages. Once separated, these scripts can test for their own dependencies and judge whether or not they should run based on the browsing environment and the page they are to interact with.

The `select`-based navigation script we just walked through is a good example of the first part of this concept in practice; it is completely self-contained. It does not, however, properly test for its numerous dependencies, the first of which is the availability of jQuery. To do that, we would need to wrap the whole thing in a conditional:

```
if ( typeof( jQuery ) != 'undefined' ) {
  // Existing code goes here
}
```

In this brief bit of code, we are checking for the existence of the `jQuery` object, which is created when jQuery (the library) is present, by checking to see that its type is not "undefined." Dependency testing is a useful strategy because it helps you avoid throwing errors in the browser and it can help speed up the user's browsing experience by not executing code unnecessarily.

Here's another simple example that may prove more familiar to you:

```
if ( document.getElementById ) {
  // Code using document.getElementById() goes here
}
```

In this case, we're making sure the DOM traversal method `document.getElementById` exists before we execute code that uses it. You probably recall us using this strategy in the event delegation example when testing for `event.preventDefault`.

Returning to the jQuery test, we can take the test a step farther and check for a specific version of jQuery. This form of testing can be useful if your script uses a method not available in earlier versions of the library. In many cases, it's smarter to test for the existence of specific methods, but version checking can be really helpful when a new release of the library substantially changes the API for a pre-existing method:

```
if ( typeof( jQuery ) != 'undefined' &&
    parseFloat( jQuery.fn.jquery ) >= 1.4 ) {
  /* Existing code that requires jQuery 1.4 or higher
     goes here */
}
```

Testing for dependencies is a great way to ensure you don't execute code that could throw errors and, the earlier you test, the more memory and processing time you can save a user who won't benefit from the script in the first place.

jQuery isn't the only dependency the script has though; as you may recall, we took its markup dependencies into account when we tested the lengths of both the `$old_nav` and `$links` collections:

```
if ( $old_nav.length && $links.length ) {
```

With this test in place, the script quietly exits when it has nothing to do and it doesn't bother creating any new elements or assigning any event handlers that are destined to go unused.

Following on this example, you can likely see myriad scenarios where investigation into the browsing environment and the page setup can help a script to determine whether or not it should run. Object existence, markup dependencies, method availability, cookie availability, and Ajax support are all ripe for the plucking. It's trivial to add code that allows a script to quietly turn itself off when any of its dependencies are not available, so there's really no reason not to do it.

If you think about it, the concept of dependency testing is quite similar to using media queries in CSS. And, speaking of CSS, we should talk about how to best manage the interaction between scripts and style.

WORKING WITH STYLE

One script dependency we haven't discussed yet is CSS. Nine times out of ten, if you are writing JavaScript that interacts with the DOM, you're also working with CSS in one way or another. When developing with progressive enhancement in mind, it's important to determine the best way to apply and control styles from within JavaScript so you don't confuse your users by creating interfaces that don't actually work. But more on that in a moment.

Over the years, our understanding of how JavaScript and CSS should interact has evolved considerably. In the early days of JavaScript, style management in a script was pretty much nonexistent; we just wrote everything inline by manipulating an element's `style` attribute:

```
function highlight() {
  var el = document.getElementById( 'message' );
  el.style.color = '#f00';
  el.style.backgroundColor = '#ffcfcf';
}
```

From a maintenance perspective, code written in this manner is a nightmare to work with. It means any time there's a design change, you need to get someone who understands JavaScript involved. That's hardly efficient and violates the separation of layers; mixing presentation and behavior makes both of them harder to work with.

The next step in the evolution was extracting the changeable bits to variables, either within the script itself or passing them in as part of a configuration object (keeping a sensible default in case the configuration was skipped):

```
function highlight( config ) {
  var el = document.getElementById( 'message' );
  el.style.color = config.color || '#f00';
  el.style.backgroundColor = config.backgroundColor
                             || '#ffcfcf';
}

highlight({
  color: '#ebebeb',
  backgroundColor: 'black'
});
```

It still requires at least a cursory knowledge of JavaScript to update the strings, but hopefully all of the style rules would be in one place, so the maintenance should be a bit easier.

Eventually, however, we realized it was much more efficient to maintain style information in an external stylesheet and trigger it by manipulating the class of an element on the page:

```
function highlight() {
  document.getElementById( 'message' )
    .className += ' highlight';
}
```

Not only did this reduce the amount of code necessary to accomplish the desired effect, but it also meant fewer DOM manipulations (which increased performance tremendously) and it meant the CSS could be maintained without modifying the JavaScript that would be interacting with those styles.

I'm going to forgo a discussion of the different ways you can bundle your scripts and styles together while still maintaining a decent amount of separation, in favor of spending some time on when and how to best apply styles using a script. While the former is certainly an interesting topic,[12] the route you choose to go has more to do with your work flow and overall project needs. When and how your scripts apply styles, however, is of critical importance and is the subject of my final maxim for progressive enhancement with JavaScript:

3. Apply no style before its time.

As we've already covered, most DOM scripting requires a bit of style modification as well—whether it's to expand and collapse an element on the page, highlight newly added content, or provide visual flourishes to a drag and drop interface. Using style in this manner is perfectly legitimate, but, more often than not, developers apply styles that correspond to a given widget before they have determined if the widget can even run.

Let's take, for example, an accordion widget. In a typical accordion interface, the content blocks are hidden and only

---

12. For an overview of that topic, you can read my article "Keeping the hot side hot and the cold side cold" in Scroll Magazine: http://scrollmagazine.com/number-1/keeping-the-hot-side-hot.

the associated headings are visible. If the styles applied to hide the content sections were applied by default and the script was unable to run, a user would be unable to click a header to reveal the hidden content. The styles would have undermined the usefulness of the interface because they were applied too early.

If, on the other hand, the script itself were to trigger the application of the initial state styles when it knew it would be able to run, there would not be any problem whatsoever. If the script didn't run, the widget-related styles would not be applied and the content would still be visible and, thereby, usable. Implementing the style application in this way, you provide one layout for the content when the widget can't run and another set of styles when it can, optimizing both use cases.

Could it be? Why yes, I think it is. Progressive enhancement perfection.

Figure 4.6: *An accordion widget showing the first section expanded and the other three sections collapsed. Clicking the title of another section will cause that section to expand and the first section to collapse.*

One of the best ways to manage triggering interface styles like this is by using an "activator" `class` on the root element of the widget. Here are some quick examples:

STRATEGY	"RESTING" CLASS	"ACTIVATED" CLASS
Add a suffix of "-on" to the base `class`	`.accordion`	`.accordion-on`
Add another `class`	`.auto-submit`	`.auto-submit.active`
Change the form of the `class`	`.replace-me`	`.replaced`

Table 4.1: *Using an "activator"* `class`.

By following this practice, you can guarantee that no styles will be applied before they are needed.

Another issue with style application by JavaScript is the potential for collisions. Just as it is important to isolate your scripts from one another to avoid collisions in variable, function, or method naming, it is recommended that you isolate your script-related styles from others as well. After all, you may not be able to control what other `class` names may be in use on a given page (especially if you're releasing a script for other people to use) and if you don't carefully sequester your styles, they can unintentionally "bleed" onto the rest of the page (i.e., they might be applied to elements you didn't intend them to apply to).

To corral your styles, it's best to start every selector with an identifiable marker unlikely to be in conflict with another `class` or `id` on the page. I like to begin with the name of the JavaScript object. So, for example, if I built an accordion widget named (cleverly) `AccordionWidget`, I might classify the activated root element as "AccordionWidget-on" and then tree each of my styles from there:

```
.AccordionWidget-on .heading {
  /* Heading styles here */
}

.AccordionWidget-on .content-block {
  /* Content block styles here */
}

.AccordionWidget-on .content-block.collapsed {
  /* Collapsed content block styles here */
}
```

Obviously, there is an outside chance that style rules intended for content other than your widget could end up bleeding into the widget as well because of issues regarding specificity or the cascade. If you anticipate those potential issues, however, you can take the appropriate action by increasing the specificity of your selectors or by explicitly setting each and every property you want to control within your widget.

PLANNING AND RESTRAINT

Make no mistake, progressive enhancement with JavaScript requires considerably more effort than it does with CSS or HTML. With a bit of thoughtful reflection and consideration of the numerous factors that affect the web experience, however, it quickly becomes second nature. And, when in doubt, you can always come back to the three maxims:

1. Make sure all content is accessible and all necessary tasks can be completed without JavaScript turned on.
2. Use JavaScript to generate any additional markup it needs.
3. Apply no style before its time.

Armed with a solid understanding of how to best wield the power of JavaScript, you're sure to make smart decisions and build even more usable sites.

"It takes many good deeds to build a good reputation, and only one bad one to lose it."

— BENJAMIN FRANKLIN

CHAPTER 5:
PROGRESSIVE ENHANCEMENT FOR ACCESSIBILITY

In February of 2006, the National Federation of the Blind took legal action against Target for having an inaccessible website. A month later the case went to federal court (at Target's request). Target tried to get the case thrown out, but it didn't fly and the case turned into a class action lawsuit that Target eventually settled in 2008 for over $6 million US (not counting attorney fees). That's pretty substantial considering that the reason the lawsuit was filed in the first place was because Target didn't fix accessibility issues they were alerted to: lack of alt text on images, heavy use of image maps, and reliance on a mouse for the submission of forms. All of these issues could have been addressed quickly and easily for far less than $6 million. Hell, I'd have done it for a few grand.

If you haven't had a lot of exposure to accessibility—with respect to this chapter, a measure of how well a site can be

used by people with disabilities and the assistive technologies[1]
they rely on—as a design consideration, it can seem incredibly
daunting because there are so many factors to consider. Even if
you fall into a category of users with "special needs," it's likely
your experience and aptitudes are different from someone
else with similar concerns. For example, you may have
deuteranopia (a type of red-green color blindness), but yours
may not be as extreme as someone else's. You also may not be
as likely to recognize potential issues for people with tritanopia
(blue-yellow color blindness).

If you're the kind of person who is concerned with issues
of accessibility, whether from the position of getting your
message to as many people as possible or because you don't
want to make someone feel left out, the self-imposed pressure
to "get it right" can seem so intense that you can't help but
approach it with trepidation.

Thankfully, designing and developing with progressive
enhancement improves accessibility. Progressive enhancement
encourages you to build your websites in service of the content
and that, more often than not, will help guide you toward the
right decision when it comes to accessibility. Of course there's
always room for improvement, hence this chapter.

NOW YOU SEE ME...

Perhaps the most heavily-repeated pattern in JavaScript-
based page manipulation is showing and hiding content.
Tabbed interfaces. Collapsible elements. Accordion widgets.
It crops up nearly everywhere. In and of itself, this pattern is
not a bad thing, but few people realize how profoundly your

---

1.   Assistive technologies come in many forms. Blind people who use
     screen-reading software. People with partially impaired vision may
     enlarge text in the browser. The deaf often rely on captioning to
     easily follow videos.

choice of hiding mechanism can influence the accessibility of your content to assistive technologies like screen readers.

When it comes to hiding content, there are several mechanisms for doing it and each has a different affect on the page, as summarized in the table below.

CSS RULES	DISPLAY EFFECT	ACCESSIBILITY EFFECT
`visibility: hidden;`	Element is hidden from view, but is not removed from the normal flow (i.e., it still takes up the space it normally would)	Content is ignored by screen readers
`display: none;`	Element is removed from the normal flow and hidden; the space it occupied is collapsed	Content is ignored by screen readers
`height: 0; width: 0; overflow: hidden;`	Element is collapsed and contents are hidden	Content is ignored by screen readers
`text-indent: -999em;`	Contents are shifted off-screen and hidden from view, but links may "focus" oddly and negative indent may not prove long enough to fully hide content	Screen readers have access to the content, but the content is limited to text and inline elements
`position: absolute; left: -999em;`	Content is removed from the normal flow and shifted off the left-hand edge; the space it occupied is collapsed	Screen readers have access to the content

Table 5.1: *Mechanisms for hiding content.*

The first two mechanisms are probably the most popular, with `display: none;` being the go-to option implemented by nearly every JavaScript library on the planet and the lion's share of ready-made JavaScript widgets. If you don't want your hidden content to be read by a screen reader, those defaults may work for you, but if you want to ensure users have access to content (even if it isn't displayed visually in the current interface), the final option is really the way to go.

If you roll your own JavaScript library, positioning content off-screen to hide it is pretty easy to implement. If, however, you are using a third-party JavaScript library, such as jQuery or Prototype, this task becomes much more difficult to accomplish because making the change requires overwriting or otherwise changing the internals of the library. Unless, of course, you're smart about how you do it.

Most libraries include, as part of their animation suite, a mechanism for including what are referred to as "callback functions." A callback function is a function that you supply to another function (or object method) so it can be called at a predetermined time. If you've used JavaScript to load content via Ajax, you're probably familiar with the concept: callback functions are used to do something with the data you got back from the server.

In most cases, JavaScript libraries only offer a callback function that runs at the completion of a given activity, but some libraries also provide hooks for various other points during the execution of a given routine, such as before the routine begins. Even without additional callback hooks, however, it's possible to create more accessible show/hide operations. Take the following jQuery-based snippet, for example:

```
(function(){
  var $button = $('#myButton'),
    $text  = $('#myText'),
    visible = true;
```

```
  $button.click(function(){
    if ( visible ) {
      $text.slideUp('fast');
    } else {
      $text.slideDown('fast');
    }
    visible = ! visible;
  });
})();
```

This script finds two elements (#myButton and #myText),
assigning them to two local variables ($button and $text,
respectively) before setting a third local variable (visible)
to track the current state of things. It then goes on to assign
an onclick event handler to #myButton that toggles
the visibility of #myText by adjusting its height. Pretty
straightforward, right?

This script works as you'd expect, but jQuery currently uses
display: none when you call slideUp(), so #myText is
being hidden via a method that prohibits the hidden text
from being read by a screen reader. By making a subtle
tweak to the code, however, we can trigger the addition of a
class we control that provides for a more accessible means
of hiding content:

```
(function(){
  var $button = $('#myButton'),
      $text   = $('#myText'),
      visible = true;
  $button.click(function(){
    if ( visible ) {
      $text.slideUp('fast',function(){
        $text.addClass('accessibly-hidden')
          .slideDown(0);
      });
    } else {
      $text.slideUp(0,function(){
```

```
    $text.removeClass('accessibly-hidden')
        .slideDown('fast');
   });
  }
  visible = ! visible;
 });
})();
```

This script is almost identical to the last one, in that when the content is being hidden, the library is allowed to manage the animation, but then the script swaps the default completion state for our custom class "accessibly-hidden," thereby keeping the content available to assistive technologies. When the script goes to show the content, the steps are reversed, with the content being hidden by the script again before the class is removed and the actual animation is performed.

The added benefit of this approach is that you control the method of hiding content completely, as opposed to leaving it up to the JavaScript library. That means you can upgrade your "accessibly-hidden" class to use a different technique if something better comes along and you don't have to wait for the library to upgrade its hiding mechanism (if it ever does).

Of course all of this assumes you want to hide content from being displayed, but you want to keep it available to older assistive devices. If, however, you don't want the content to be read by a screen reader, you *could* use display: none, but it's still not the best route to go because there's no easy way to let the user know new content is available if you ever want to show that content. To really provide the best experience for you users, you'll want to employ the roles and states defined in the Web Accessibility Initiative's Accessible Rich Internet Applications spec (WAI-ARIA or ARIA, for short).[2]

---

2. http://www.w3.org/TR/wai-aria/

Hiding content with ARIA is pretty straightforward: you simply employ the `aria-hidden` attribute.

```
<p aria-hidden="true">Guess what? I'm accessibly
  hidden using ARIA.</p>
```

ARIA offers a number of predefined roles, states, and properties that can be of tremendous use when building a JavaScript-heavy site. There are even a handful that are useful whether you are building a highly interactive application or not. We'll tackle those first.

EMPOWER WAYFINDING

One of the many ways ARIA helps improve the accessibility of a web page is through the use of "landmark" and "structural" roles. Many of these roles formalize the significance we had been attempting to impart to elements for years via by applying semantic classifications and identifiers (as we discussed in Chapter 2). ARIA's landmark and structural roles (and widget roles, which we'll get to shortly) are assigned to an element using the `role` attribute.

I know, I know: `role` isn't a valid attribute in HTML 4.x or XHTML 1.x. It's true. ARIA adds a host of new attributes to the HTML lexicon, which means you won't be able to validate your pages using the same old Document Type Definitions (DTDs) you've been using. If you want to validate your ARIA-infused pages in either of these two languages, you'll need to use a different set of DTDs[3] or make the leap to HTML5 which supports attributes like `role`.

---

3. The HTML 4.01 plus WAI-ARIA `DOCTYPE` is `<!DOCTYPE html PUBLIC "-//W3C//DTD HTML+ARIA 1.0//EN" "http://www.w3.org/WAI/ARIA/schemata/html4-aria-1.dtd">`. The XHTML plus WAI-ARIA `DOCTYPE` is `<!DOCTYPE html PUBLIC "-//W3C//DTD XHTML+ARIA 1.0//EN" "http://www.w3.org/WAI/ARIA/schemata/xhtml-aria-1.dtd">`.

Here's a quick example of ARIA in action:

```
<ol role="navigation">
  <li><a href="#details">Details</a></li>
  <li><a href="#schedule">Schedule</a></li>
  <li><a href="#instructors">Instructors</a></li>
  <li><a href="#lodging">Lodging</a></li>
  <li><a href="#location">Location</a></li>
</ol>
```

You should recognize this bit of markup from Chapter 2; it's the navigation for the Retreats 4 Geeks page. The only difference between this and our original markup is that the ol now has a role attribute with a value of "navigation." As you'd suspect, the ARIA landmark "navigation" role denotes that an element is acting as a navigational mechanism.

All of ARIA's landmark roles convey information about regions of the page itself and are useful for overall page navigation. Some assistive technologies expose these landmarks to users, allowing them to directly move from region to region via keystrokes or other means. They are the logical successor to a bevy of "skip to" links.[4] Structural roles, on the other hand, act as organizational tools akin to HTML5 elements like section and article.

You may recall that, in the original example, we wrapped the navigational ol in a new HTML5 element: nav. If you are really on the ball, you'll also recall that using the nav element is semantically-equivalent to employing the landmark role "navigation." And this isn't the only area of overlap between HTML5 and ARIA.

---

4. "Skip to" links are links that provide anchor-based access to regions of a page. Common implementations include "Skip to content" and "Skip to navigation." They were a mainstay of the web standards world for many years, but ARIA's landmark roles make these links redundant.

Redundancy and reason

These two specs developed independently over roughly the same time period and each sought to address the pressing problems they saw with the current state of HTML. (Hence, the inevitable overlap.) The ARIA spec is currently a bit closer to becoming a recommendation than HTML5 is and, as a consequence, many of its unique features are being incorporated into HTML5 as that spec continues to develop. When HTML5 finally reaches the Candidate Recommendation stage, it's pretty safe to assume that the two specs will have been successfully merged and that redundancies will have been ironed out.

For the time being, however, there is a considerable amount of overlap between ARIA and HTML5, especially in the case of structural and (to a lesser extent) landmark roles. Table 5.2 provides a few examples of our traditional ad-hoc semantics, their equivalent ARIA role, and the HTML5 element (if any) that serves the same purpose.

AD-HOC SEMANTICS	ARIA ROLE	HTML5 ELEMENT	SEMANTIC MEANING
`#header,` `#top`	banner	header (kind of)	A region of the page that is site-focused, rather than page-focused
`#main,` `#content`	main	none	The focal content in a document

Table 5.2: *Traditional ad-hoc semantics, their equivalent ARIA role, and the HTML5 element (if any) that serves the same purpose.*

AD-HOC SEMANTICS	ARIA ROLE	HTML5 ELEMENT	SEMANTIC MEANING
`#extra,` `.sidebar`	complemen-tary, note	`aside`	A supporting section of the document that is related to the main content ("complementary" content remains meaningful when separated from it)
`#footer,` `#bottom`	contentinfo	`footer`	A region that contains information about the document
`#nav`	navigation	`nav`	A region of the page containing navigational links
`.hentry`	article	`article`	A region of the page that forms an independent part of the document

Table 5.2: *Traditional ad-hoc semantics, their equivalent ARIA role, and the HTML5 element (if any) that serves the same purpose.*

At present, there is a bit of back-and-forth between the HTML5 community and accessibility advocates over what to do about the redundancy. From a practical standpoint, even if you are using HTML5's ARIA-equivalent semantics it's generally considered a good idea to double up with the ARIA landmark roles because not all assistive technologies are HTML5-aware yet. Structural roles, however, can be assigned at your own discretion as they are purely organizational and are not currently exposed to users via assistive technology.

A quick scan of the Retreats 4 Geeks source code will reveal this redundancy on the `nav` and `footer` elements. As assistive technologies are updated to be HTML5-compatible, however, we will be able to jettison the unnecessary role attributes and streamline our markup a bit more.

In addition to overlap with HTML5, there are quite a few roles that duplicate the semantics long available in HTML. Consider the following ARIA landmark and structural roles: columnheader, definition, form, heading, img, list, listitem, row, rowheader, and separator. Some of those have one-to-one equivalencies in HTML (e.g., "form") and the others are a more generalized form of what we have in HTML (e.g., "list").

While it's understandable that the parallel development of ARIA and HTML5 would create some overlap, you may be scratching your head over why ARIA would seem to recreate semantics that have existed in HTML for over a decade. The simple answer is that, for one reason or another, some companies (`<cough>Google</cough>`) like to use non-semantic markup (e g , `div`s) as the basis for an interface and use JavaScript to make it function like a native HTML control. For that reason alone, ARIA provides overlapping roles. You won't see me running out to give a `div` a role of "form" (I'll just use a `form`, thank you), but to each his own I guess.

As we discussed earlier, the Retreats 4 Geeks site implements several of the HTML5 elements that are semantically-equivalent to ARIA's landmark and structural roles—`nav`, `footer`, `article`—but we've opted to include the equivalent ARIA roles in the interest of serving the greatest number of users. (After all, that's what progressive enhancement is all about, right?) We're not done though. As we saw in Table 5.2, the semantic equivalence of an ARIA role of "banner" to HTML5's `header` is somewhat debatable so, to be absolutely clear in the service of our users, I've added that role as well:

```
<header role="banner">
```

The only other role we haven't touched on (since it's currently not addressed in HTML5) is "main," which indicates the focal content of the document. You may recall from Chapter 2 that I chose a `section` element to enclose the various `articles` on the page and that it was also the element I chose to act as the root of our hCalendar; that `section` just screams "main" to me:

```
<section id="content" class="vevent" role="main">
```

And with those two minor adjustments, we've covered every landmark role that seems sensible to employ on the Retreats 4 Geeks site. Not only that, but we've improved the overall accessibility of our page by providing easy ways for users of assistive technology to move around the document.

BROTHER CAN YOU SPARE A CLUE?

In addition to providing users with a means to find their way around a document, the ARIA spec prescribes other helpful tools as well, not the least of which is its collection of widget roles and states.

Widget roles do just what you'd expect them to: describe the role of a given element. These roles are generally divided into two camps: roles that provide a defined structure, and those that don't. Or, more simply, containers and components. Containers are the elements that house the components of a given widget.

Consider the tabbed interface shown in Figure 5.1. A tabbed interface is constructed from two component parts: a list of tabs and a collection of panels shown by those tabs. Those parts break down into three separate roles in the ARIA spec: the tabs themselves have a `role` of "tab," the list of tabs has a `role` of "tablist," and each panel is assigned a role of "tabpanel." In terms of designations, both "tab" and "tabpanel" are considered component roles, while "tablist" is considered a container role (because it contains the tabs).

Pumpkin Pie

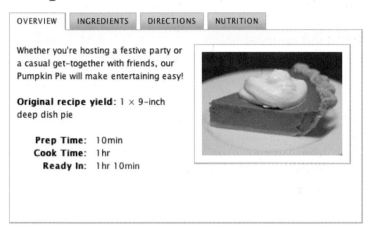

Photo by *Paul Goyette*, licensed under *Creative Commons*.

Figure 5.1: *A tabbed interface.*

The ARIA spec defines a number of widget roles, making it possible to construct anything from complex form controls (e.g., sliders and spinner boxes) to tree-based menus, modal dialog boxes, and drag-and-drop interfaces, all while maintaining accessibility. And, as with the structural roles we discussed earlier, ARIA even provides mechanisms for redefining nonsense markup as something functional:

```
<div role="button">I&#8217;m not a real button, but
    I play one on the web</div>
```

Of course all of this is well and good, but for any widget to work you need JavaScript and, traditionally, that's been an accessibility no man's land. The main reason that techniques like Ajax and accessibility didn't mesh well was that the HTML language provided no mechanism by which JavaScript could update the user (or her assistive technology of choice) in real-time beyond alert() and confirm() (which, let's face it, are the hooligans at the back of the user interface classroom).

The ARIA spec addresses issues of context with what are called "states." ARIA states are a set of attributes that can be applied to nearly any element. Some are global in scope (i.e., they can be applied to any element), while others are specific to certain widget contexts. All are prefaced with "aria-" and they provide valuable information to the user about what is going on with a given element.

Guess what? You're already familiar with one: `aria-hidden`. The `aria-hidden` attribute we discussed earlier in this chapter accepts a boolean ("true" or "false") value and lets the user agent or assistive technology know whether or not the content within should be exposed to the user. Other examples of ARIA states include `aria-disabled`, `aria-expanded`, `aria-invalid`, `aria-pressed`, and `aria-selected`.

In terms of the tabbed interface from Figure 5.1, the states we'd likely want to employ would be `aria-hidden` for the state of the tab panels and `aria-selected` for the state of the tabs themselves.

But the ARIA spec doesn't stop there. In addition to state-indicative attributes, it also defines numerous properties that can be set on an element. Examples include `aria-autocomplete`, `aria-controls`, `aria-label`, `aria-labelledby`, `aria-readonly`, and `aria-required`. As you can see, most of the properties are meant for use with form controls, but a few (like `aria-controls`) can apply to our tabbed interface.

As you probably suspect, the `aria-controls` takes an `id` reference for a value and that `id` should belong to the element whose contents or presence is controlled by the element to which the attribute is applied. In the case of the tabbed interface, the tab would "control" its associated tab panel (as shown in Figure 5.2). With the tab-to-tab-panel relationship established, it seems only fair to establish the relationship in the other direction as well; that's where

`aria-labelledby` can be put to use. It works in precisely
the same way as `aria-controls`.

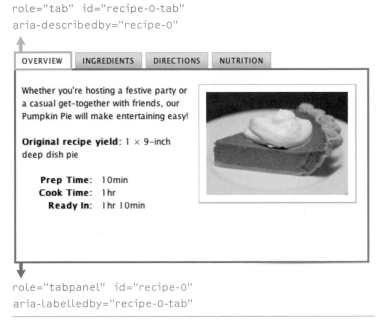

```
role="tab" id="recipe-0-tab"
aria-describedby="recipe-0"
```

```
role="tabpanel" id="recipe-0"
aria-labelledby="recipe-0-tab"
```

Figure 5.2: *Using ARIA properties, we can relate pieces of an interface to
one another.*

ARIA's states and properties go a long way toward helping
keep the user informed, but few concepts in ARIA are as
simple and immediately useful as Live Regions.

IT'S ALIVE!

With the advent of Ajax and the resurgence of JavaScript in
general, few things proved to be more of a user experience
nightmare than live-updating regions of the page. The
usability issues were numerous, but the two big ones were:
1) assistive devices weren't aware of changes to the page
and had no way of directing a user's attention to them; and

2) users taking advantage of page zoom or browsing on a mobile device are oblivious to content updates occurring off-screen. Thankfully, the ARIA spec includes an attribute that directly addresses this egregious problem: `aria-live`.

What's most exciting about `aria-live` is its simplicity. By applying this single attribute to an element, you can control how and when content updates within it are presented to your users. The `aria-live` attribute accepts one of three values:

1. "off" for when updates are frequent and of little importance to the user, as in the case of a live stream from your Twitter account (doh!);
2. "polite" for when updates are only important enough to be announced when the user isn't doing anything, as in the case of updated news headlines; or
3. "assertive" for when updates are important enough to announce immediately, as in the case of form validation messages.

In the Retreats 4 Geeks website, it makes sense to apply `aria-live` to the contact form:

```
<article id="contact" aria-live="assertive">
```

With that in place, users will be kept abreast of any errors encountered when filling in their details and will also be informed when the submission is successful.

SUPPORT AND STUMBLING BLOCKS

Since its introduction, ARIA has gotten a lot of support from the web community. As of this writing, some level of ARIA support is found in every major browser and has been implemented in popular screen reading tools like JAWS, Windows Eyes, NVDA, and Orca. Influential companies like IBM, Sun Microsystems, Adobe, Yahoo!, and Google are all working diligently to increase ARIA's effectiveness and reach. Even the JavaScript community has embraced ARIA, with both Dojo Dijits[5] and jQuery UI[6] integrating ARIA's roles, states, and properties into their components. Of course, the spec is still developing, so no implementation is complete, but progress is being made.

I'd be remiss if I did not mention the one major issue keeping ARIA from fitting neatly into the progressive enhancement stack, at least when it comes to widget-related roles and states: we have no way of testing for ARIA support in the browser or assistive technology and, therefore, can't make informed decisions about how to best implement a given widget. Derek Featherstone surfaced this issue in his excellent article for *A List Apart* Entitled "ARIA and Progressive Enhancement."[7] I highly recommend reading it to better understand the issue. At the time of this writing, a viable solution has not been proposed, but my fingers are crossed.

KEYSTROKE ISN'T A DIRTY WORD

The last topic I want to touch on before we wrap this, the final chapter of my little book, is keyboard access and controls. With the pervasiveness of the mouse and an increased reliance on touch-based devices like the iPad, it is relatively easy to forget about the humble keyboard, but that would be a critical mistake. The keyboard is an incredibly useful tool and is the standard interface for all non-visual users and most power-users.

When it comes to the keyboard, we've learned a great deal in the last few years. First off, we realized that access keys were a good idea in theory, but not so great in practice.[8] Second,

---

5. http://dojotoolkit.org/widgets

6. http://jqueryui.com/

7. http://alistapart.com/articles/aria-and-progressive-enhancement/

8. http://www.wats.ca/show.php?contentid=32

we realized that overzealous application of the `tabindex` attribute could get your users jumping (and not in a good way).[9] But the most important thing we discovered is that we could use JavaScript to "juggle" the `tabindex` attribute to streamline a user's path through a complex widget like a tabbed interface or an accordion form.

So what exactly is `tabindex` juggling? Well, some time in 2005 (it's hard to pin down the exact origin) it was discovered that assigning a value of "-1" to the `tabindex` attribute of an element would remove that element from the default tab order of the document.[10] Interestingly, despite being taken out of the document's tab order, the element remained focusable via JavaScript (`element.focus()`), which opened up a lot of possibilities for controlling a user's experience.

Let's walk through a scenario, revisiting the tabbed interface from earlier:

1. A user arrives at the tabbed interface and clicks the `tab` key on her keyboard, bringing focus to the first tab (which is associated with the visible tab panel).

2. Clicking the `tab` button again moves focus out of the tab interface to the next piece of focusable content instead of taking her to the next tab in the list.

3. Holding `shift` while hitting the `tab` key brings the user back into the tab list and restores focus to the currently active tab.

4. Using the arrow keys, she can move forward and backward through the tabs in the tab list, bringing each associated tab panel into view as she moves.

5. Hitting the `enter` button at any point while navigating through the tab list brings focus to the tab panel associated with that tab.

---

9. http://webaim.org/techniques/keyboard/tabindex

10. This was especially interesting because, according to the W3C spec, `tabindex` should only accept values between 0 and 32767.

I know that's a lot of "tabs" (and a bit of a tall order), but with tabindex juggling and a little JavaScript it becomes quite simple to achieve. Here's how:

1. By assigning a tabindex of "-1" to every tab and tab panel, you can remove them from the tab order of the page.

2. Going back and re-assigning a value of "0" to the currently active tab restores their default position in the tab order.

3. Using JavaScript you can dynamically adjust the tabindex property of each tab as a user executes keyboard commands like left or right, up or down, allowing the user to move quickly and easily through the interface.

Here's a snippet from TabInterface's swap method that shows tabindex juggling in action (along with some ARIA attribute manipulation and class swapping):

```
function swap( e ) {
  // ...
  // De-activating the current tab & tab panel
  removeClassName( old_tab, 'active' );
  old_tab.setAttribute( 'aria-selected', 'false' );
  old_tab.setAttribute( 'tabindex', '-1' );
  removeClassName( old_folder, 'visible' );
  old_folder.setAttribute( 'aria-hidden', 'true' );
  // Activating the new tab & tab panel
  addClassName( tab, 'active' );
  tab.setAttribute( 'aria-selected', 'true' );
  tab.setAttribute( 'tabindex', '0' );
  addClassName( new_folder, 'visible' );
  new_folder.setAttribute( 'aria-hidden', 'false' );
  // ...
}
```

If you'd like to see this technique in action, you can check out TabInterface.js on Github.[11]

---

11. http://github.com/easy-designs/TabInterface.js

JUST DO IT... ACCESSIBLY

Accessibility is complex and can be difficult to wrap your mind around, but if you tackle it a little at a time, it becomes second nature. And, as with everything else in this book, accessibility is most easily applied in layers, building up the interface bit by bit to create something that meets your users' needs, whatever they may be.

"If you want to build a ship, don't drum up the men to gather wood, divide the work and give orders. Instead, teach them to yearn for the vast and endless sea."

— ANTOINE DE SAINT-EXUPERY

CHAPTER 6:
TAKE IT AWAY

In our brief time together, we've covered a lot of ground. We witnessed progressive enhancement in action, tracing the development of a simple text document into a beautiful, functional, and accessible web page. It was a whirlwind journey to be sure, but hopefully you are coming away from it with a better picture of what progressive enhancement is, why it works, and how to incorporate it into your design and development process. Perhaps you've even picked up a few useful techniques that you'll be able to apply in your own projects.

Even though this is a short book and we have an excellent indexer, it's easy to forget where you saw something useful. To assist with that, I've provided a summary of the book's techniques below, with a brief description and the page on which to read more about them.

I have also compiled a progressive enhancement checklist that you can use (and share with your colleagues) to help you make sure you've given proper consideration to the most important aspects of progressive enhancement. Assuming you don't want to ruin this book by tearing out the page, you can download the checklist at http://easy-readers.net/books/adaptive-web-design/checklist.pdf.

Now get out there and make something great!

THE PROGRESSIVE ENHANCEMENT CHECKLIST

Content & HTML

☐ Author copy that is well-written and makes sense when read aloud
This is the baseline experience for every user and it matters. It is briefly discussed on page 13, but for more, see Further Reading later in this chapter.

☐ Choose semantically-appropriate elements
Using the existing semantics in HTML does wonders for accessibility (and search engine optimization). A discussion of semantic HTML begins on page 19.

☐ Use Microformats to fortify HTML's gaps
Microformats are extensions to the HTML lexicon and are supported by numerous browsers and several search engines. Microformats were introduced on page 29.

☐ Use classification to group elements serving the same function
Classification (i.e., using the `class` attribute) helps convey meaning about elements when HTML's inherent semantics fail you and no microformats fit the bill. Classification is introduced on page 25.

☐ Identify landmark elements
Identification (i.e., using the `id` attribute) is a great way to give context to specific regions of a page or specific instances of a classified element. Identification is discussed on page 25.

CSS

☐ Double check your compound selectors

Mixing selectors of vastly different complexity can cause issues when a browser doesn't understand one of them: the entire rule set will be ignored. If your intent is to hide the rule set from older browsers, however, this can be a useful tactic. This topic was introduced on page 50.

☐ Organize your CSS rules with the cascade in mind

Order matters and proper organization of your style rules can help you create a progressive design and make your CSS more maintainable. A refresher on the cascade and how it can be used to great effect begins on page 52.

☐ Hide groups of advanced CSS rule sets from older browsers

One of the most powerful tools available in CSS for hiding rule sets *en masse* is by using @media blocks. A discussion of using @media in this manner begins on page 59.

☐ Use Conditional Comments to handle IE issues

Older versions of IE are notoriously buggy and Conditional Comments are the best way to provide CSS and JavaScript patches to specific versions of IE. They work best in the "trickle-down" pattern. Conditional Comments were discussed on page 62.

☐ Make sure you've accounted for alternate media and contexts

Media assignment and media queries can be used to deliver tailored layouts and experiences based on the user's context. A discussion of these topics begins on page 64.

JavaScript

☐ Ensure all JavaScript is "unobtrusive"

Scripts should be maintained as far from the markup as possible and should be as generic as possible. This allows you to re-factor them independently. Your JavaScripts should not be tied to specific markup, but be flexible enough to adapt as your pages evolve. Unobtrusive JavaScript was introduced on page 78.

☐ Make sure all content is accessible and all necessary tasks can be completed without JavaScript turned on
You can't rely on JavaScript. Period. If you want to enhance with JavaScript, follow the Hijax pattern. A discussion of Hijax begins on page 80.

☐ Use JavaScript to generate any additional markup it needs
JavaScript is great at manipulating the DOM, so there's no reason to hard-code markup into a page that is only there for your script's benefit. For more on DOM manipulation, see page 83.

☐ Use JavaScript to enable script-related styles
There are few things as annoying as content being organized into a widget and having the widget not work because JavaScript is turned off or there's an error in the script. Use a switch to allow JavaScript to turn widget-related styles on. For more on CSS switches, revisit page 93.

☐ Delivered scripts *à la carte* whenever possible
Any script that can run independently should be designed to do so, with its own set of tests to determine whether or not it can run. For more on *à la carte* script delivery, see page 90.

Accessibility

☐ Use ARIA landmarks where appropriate
If you're using HTML5, some ARIA landmarks may seem redundant, but it's better to have too cover your bases. It's trivial to use them and they can greatly improve the accessibility of a page. A discussion of AIRA landmark roles begins on page 106.

☐ Use ARIA roles and states to provide users with more detail about widgets

When you create a widget using JavaScript, there are very few ways to provide users with valuable information about what is happening when they are interacting with it. Roles and states fill in the blanks. A discussion of roles and states begins on page 111.

☐ Use Tabindex to control a user's journey through the page

Using the `tabindex` attribute, you carve a path through your page, bringing users to the important landmarks quickly and easily. Taking it a step further, JavaScript can be used to adjust what can and cannot be focused as a user interacts with various page components. A discussion of how `tabindex` can best be used begins on page 116.

FURTHER READING

Content & Copywriting

The Elements of Content Strategy by Erin Kissane, A Book Apart, 2011

Content Strategy for the Web by Kristina Halvorson, New Riders, 2009

"Writing Content that Works for a Living" by Erin Kissane, *A List Apart* http://www.alistapart.com/articles/writingcontentthatworksforaliving/

"Reviving Anorexic Web Writing" by Amber Simmons, *A List Apart* http://www.alistapart.com/articles/revivinganorexicwebwriting/

"Better Writing Through Design" by Bronwyn Jones http://www.alistapart.com/articles/betterwritingthroughdesign/

"Calling All Designers: Learn to Write!" by Derek Powazek, *A List Apart* http://www.alistapart.com/articles/learntowrite/

"Attack of the Zombie Copy" by Erin Kissane, *A List Apart* http://www.alistapart.com/articles/zombiecopy/

Markup

HTML5 for Web Designers by Jeremy Keith, A Book Apart, 2010

Designing with Web Standards, 3rd Edition by Jeffrey Zeldman and Ethan Marcotte, New Riders, 2009

Developing with Web Standards by John Allsopp,
New Riders, 2009

Microformats: Empowering Your Markup for Web 2.0 by John
Allsopp, Friends of ED, 2007

*Web Standards Solutions: The Markup and Style Handbook,
Special Edition* by Dan Cederholm, Friends of ED, 2009

"Where Our Standards Went Wrong" by Ethan Marcotte,
A List Apart http://www.alistapart.com/articles/
whereourstandardswentwrong/

"How to Grok Web Standards" by Craig Cook, *A List Apart*
http://www.alistapart.com/articles/grok
webstandards/

"Using XHTML/CSS for an Effective SEO Campaign" by
Brandon Olejniczak, *A List Apart* http://www.alistapart.
com/articles/seo/

CSS

CSS3 for Web Designers by Dan Cederholm, A Book Apart, 2010

Handcrafted CSS: More Bulletproof Web Design by Dan
Cederholm and Ethan Marcotte, New Riders, 2009

*CSS Mastery: Advanced Web Standards Solutions, Second
Edition* by Simon Collison, Andy Budd, and Cameron Moll,
Friends of ED, 2009

*Bulletproof Web Design: Improving flexibility and protecting
against worst-case scenarios with XHTML and CSS (2nd Edition)*
by Dan Cederholm, New Riders, 2007

More Eric Meyer on CSS by Eric Meyer, New Riders, 2004

Eric Meyer on CSS: Mastering the Language of Web Design by Eric Meyer, New Riders, 2002

"Adaptive Layouts with Media Queries" by Aaron Gustafson, *.net Magazine*, Issue 205

"Responsive Web Design" by Ethan Marcotte, *A List Apart* http://www.alistapart.com/articles/responsive-web-design/

"Accessible Data Visualization with Web Standards" by Wilson Miner, *A List Apart* http://www.alistapart.com/articles/accessibledatavisualization/

"Big, Stark & Chunky" by Joe Clark, *A List Apart* http://www.alistapart.com/articles/lowvision/

"Elastic Design" by Patrick Griffiths, *A List Apart* http://www.alistapart.com/articles/elastic/

"CSS Design: Going to Print" by Eric Meyer, *A List Apart* http://www.alistapart.com/articles/goingtoprint/

JavaScript

Bulletproof Ajax by Jeremy Keith, New Riders, 2007

DOM Scripting by Jeremy Keith, Friends of ED, 2006

"Test-Driven Progressive Enhancement" by Scott Jehl, *A List Apart* http://www.alistapart.com/articles/testdriven/

"Behavioral Separation" by Jeremy Keith, *A List Apart* http://www.alistapart.com/articles/behavioralseparation/

"Improving Link Display for Print" by Aaron Gustafson, *A List Apart* http://www.alistapart.com/articles/improvingprint/

"JavaScript Triggers" by Peter Paul Koch, *A List Apart* http://www.alistapart.com/articles/scripttriggers/

Accessibility & ARIA

Designing with Progressive Enhancement: Building the Web that Works for Everyone by Todd Parker, Scott Jehl, Maggie Costello Wachs, and Patty Toland, New Riders, 2010

Just Ask: Integrating Accessibility Throughout Design by Shawn Lawton Henry, Lulu, 2007

Design Accessible Web Sites: 36 Keys to Creating Content for All Audiences and Platforms by Jeremy Sydik, Pragmatic Bookshelf, 2007

"Accessible Web 2.0 Applications with WAI-ARIA" by Martin Kliehm, *A List Apart* http://www.alistapart.com/articles/waiaria/

"HTML5 and the myth of WAI-ARIA redundance" by Steve Faulkner, *The Paciello Group Blog* http://www.paciellogroup.com/blog/?p=585

"DHTML Style Guide" by AOL Developer Network http://dev.aol.com/dhtml_style_guide

"Making Compact Forms More Accessible" by Mike Brittain, *A List Apart* http://www.alistapart.com/articles/makingcompactformsmoreaccessible/

"High Accessibility Is Effective Search Engine Optimization" by Andy Hagans, *A List Apart* http://www.alistapart.com/articles/accessibilityseo/

"What Is Web Accessibility?" by Trenton Moss, *A List Apart* http://www.alistapart.com/articles/wiwa/

INDEX

ABOUT THE AUTHOR

Aaron has been working on the web for nearly 15 years and, in that time, has cultivated a love of web standards and an in-depth knowledge of website strategy and architecture, interface design, and numerous languages (including XHTML, CSS, JavaScript, and PHP). Aaron and his wife, Kelly McCarthy, own Easy! Designs, a boutique web consultancy based in Chattanooga, TN. When not neck deep in code, Aaron is usually found evangelizing his findings and sharing his knowledge and passion with others in the field.

Aaron has trained professionals at the *New York Times*, Gartner, and the US Environmental Protection Agency (among others), and has presented at the world's foremost web conferences, such as An Event Apart and Web Directions. He is Group Manager of the Web Standards Project (WaSP) and serves as an Invited Expert to the World Wide Web Consortium's Open Web Education Alliance (OWEA). He created eCSStender, serves as Technical Editor for *A List Apart*, is a contributing writer for *.net Magazine*, and has filled a small library with his technical writing and editing credits.

ABOUT EASY READERS

Easy! Readers books are skillfully and cleverly written publications that explore best practices and web standards for seasoned and aspiring web professionals. Reigning web practitioner, Aaron Gustafson, and industry peers author a series of books that address holistic approaches to crafting top-notch websites.

With a strong focus on usability and accessibility, Easy! Readers' mission is to guide readers through the origins, philosophies and practical uses of various topics as they relate to web standards. Because the web is an ever-changing medium whose scope, audience and platform continue to change and grow, we are dedicated to bringing you content that is dynamic and relevant.

Easy Readers' books may be purchased in bulk for educational use. For more information, contact our educational sales department: education@easy-readers.net.

COLOPHON

The text is set in Fresco Plus and its companion, Fresco Sans Plus, both by Fred Smeijers. The book and chapter titles are set in Trade Gothic by Jackson Burke. Code is set in FF OCR F by Albert-Jan Pool.

We believe in supporting local business and sustainable practices. This book was printed by Starkey Printing Company in Chattanooga, Tennessee. The paper used—100lb Chorus Art Silk Cover and 80lb Chorus Art Silk Text—is FSC certified and made with 50% recycled (30% post-consumer) content.